INTERNET C·H·A·T QUICK TOUR

REAL-TIME CONVERSATIONS & COMMUNICATIONS ONLINE

DONALD ROSE

VENTANA
PRESS

Internet Chat Quick Tour: Real-Time Conversations & Communications Online
Copyright © 1995 by Donald Rose

Library of Congress Cataloging-in-Publication Data

Rose, Donald.
       Internet Chat quick tour : real-time conversations and communications online / Donald Rose.
            p. cm.
       Includes index
       ISBN 1-56604-223-2
       1. Internet Relay Chat. I. Title.
    TK5105.886.R68 1995
    302.23--dc20   95-1925
                                      CIP

Book design: Marcia Webb
Vice President, Ventana Press: Walter R. Bruce III
Art Director: Marcia Webb
Design staff: Dawne Sherman, Mike Webster
Editorial Manager: Pam Richardson
Editorial staff: Angela Anderson, Tracye Giles, Nathaniel Mund
Developmental Editor: Tim C. Mattson
Project Editor: Eric Edstam
Line Editor: Lynn Jaluvka
Print Department: Wendy Bernhardt, Dan Koeller
Product Manager: Clif McCormick
Production Manager: John Cotterman
Production staff: Lance Kozlowski
Index service: Richard T. Evans, Infodex
Proofreader: Martin V. Minner
Technical review: Gary Moore
First Edition 9 8 7 6 5 4 3 2 1

Printed in the United States of America

Ventana Press, Inc.
P.O. Box 2468
Chapel Hill, NC 27515
919/942-0220   FAX 919/942-1140

Limits of Liability and Disclaimer of Warranty

TRADEMARKS

Trademarked names appear throughout this book. Rather than list the names and entities that own the trademarks or insert a trademark symbol with each mention of the trademarked name, the publisher states that it is using the names only for editorial purposes and to the benefit of the trademark owner with no intention of infringing upon that trademark.

ABOUT THE AUTHOR

Donald Rose received his Ph.D. in computer science from the University of California at Irvine, specializing in artificial intelligence—the art and science of making machines that think. With more than a dozen technical papers on various areas of AI to his credit, Donald has lectured internationally on the subject, and he has worked in the AI departments of Hughes and Rockwell (including a stint at NASA), as well as USC's Information Science Institute.

Currently, Donald consults on a variety of computer topics, from AI to multimedia to the Internet, which he has been using for over a dozen years. He is co-author of *Internet Roadside Attractions* (Ventana Press, 1995) and author of *Minding Your Cybermanners on the Internet* (Alpha Books, 1994), a guide to Internet etiquette and folklore. He also contributed several chapters to *CyberLife!* (SAMS, 1994), a survey of future technologies.

Donald's non-technical interests include screenwriting—he has written science fiction as well as comedy scripts—and live performance (music and stand-up comedy). He'd love to host an all-science talk show one day, if anyone would listen!

ACKNOWLEDGMENTS

First, I would like to thank the wonderful group of folks I've met on IRC. In particular, my thanks to Gregor, Heloise and all the folks on #poems and #30plus for being so friendly and helpful. Much appreciation also goes to Steve Arbuss and Bob "Django" Rice for their wonderfully humorous outlook on life, and their mutual love of IRC.

I also want to thank all the folks at Ventana Press, who not only made the writing and publishing process proceed smoothly, but also happen to be some of the friendliest folks I've ever interacted with. In particular, let me single out Elizabeth Woodman, Pam Richardson, Tim Mattson and Eric Edstam for their encouragement, editorial expertise and patience. Also thanks to Luke Duncan for help with Ventana Online, and Tracye Giles for speedy, friendly assistance and excellent phone repartee.

Thanks also to Pat Langley, for always supporting and encouraging my writing; Michael Utvich for much-appreciated friendship and career guidance; Matt Wagner for being a great agent; Jeannine Parker for being...well, a swell, helpful and fun person all around; and, last but not least, my mom Jean, brother Bob and sister-in-law Elsa, for their persistent advice, humor and love.

CONTENTS

INTRODUCTION

So you love the Internet. In particular, you're all but hooked on e-mail and USENET newsgroups. And yet despite these remarkable services, you still long for something more. If only you could have an e-mail conversation with a friend or colleague in real time—more like a phone conversation than a game of phone tag. If only you could access lots of folks' opinions on a subject, like on USENET, but have these thoughts transmitted as fast as light, like a real interactive town hall of sorts.

Well, thanks to an innovative service called Internet Relay Chat (IRC for short), now you can. Using IRC, you can engage in real-time conversations with one or more people, even though each may be physically located anywhere around the globe! This book will help guide you into the world of IRC, and you'll even have some fun along the way. Among other things, the chapters to follow will help you learn

- What you must do in order to get connected to IRC.

- How to communicate within this medium.

- Which communication channels are fun or informative (even weird or wild), and how to jump onto and participate in these channels.

- What rules of etiquette apply in this subculture of the Internet, and what behavioral traits and quirks you might expect to encounter in the IRC realm.

Hardware & Software Requirements

Unfortunately, this book alone cannot get you to the promised land of IRC—you also need the right hardware and software in order to make your connection to IRC and communicate within its domain. Although this subject is covered in more detail later in the book, here is a quick survey of what hardware/software you need.

If you are accessing the Internet via a shell account that includes IRC as one of its featured services, you'll probably have few or no worries; the hardware and software you use to access your service provider should be enough to run IRC. (In fact, for these users, running IRC may be as easy as selecting a menu item or typing "irc.") However, if you have a SLIP/PPP Internet account or a direct Internet connection, you must have an IRC *client*, a software program that lets your computer "talk to" IRC in the proper manner. You can generally download one of these IRC clients from any number of sites on the Internet, or from the *Internet Chat Online Companion* (see Appendix C).

A fast modem is important, since you are communicating in real-time when you use IRC. I recommend 14.4k baud (which essentially has become the current standard) or faster. A color monitor is not required, since in most cases the interaction on IRC is text-only. When graphical interactions over IRC become more widely used, then you may want to use a color monitor, but for now this is not an issue for the vast majority of users. Any size monitor is fine, but larger screens are preferred (e.g., to read previous input from users on a channel without having to frequently scroll back to previous screens).

How to Use This Book

Some readers may feel most comfortable reading this book from cover to cover before getting onto IRC. This is certainly the safest route to take. However, I suspect that the majority of readers are fairly Net-savvy already, and hence can be more adventurous. Some of you may want to use the book more "interactively" with IRC. After reading Chapters 1 through 3, you should be able to do some brief initial IRC exploring while you continue on with the rest of the book. Still, to get the most benefit out of your IRC experience—especially if you want to find a "cool" channel right away and really know what you're doing from the start—I would recommend reading all the chapters before diving into the deep end of IRC.

What's Inside

Chapter 1, "The ABC's of IRC," gives a broad survey of IRC concepts. It covers the birth and growth of IRC, some observations on IRC's strengths as well as problems or weaknesses, a primer on IRC culture and psychology, and a look at how IRC relates to other Net services.

Chapter 2, "Getting Connected," gives instructions and tips to help you get onto IRC. Discussion topics include types of Internet connections, how to get the right kind of IRC client (the program you or your Net service provider runs in order to connect to IRC and communicate), and how to select a server (the computer that "greets" your client and allows it to access IRC).

In Chapter 3, "IRC Commands & Concepts," you'll learn more about channels, nicknames, bots and ops (operators), as well as several main commands that you'll need to be familiar with to communicate effectively on IRC. The chapter also covers how to enter, track and save text that appears on IRC channels, and some brief advice for your initial IRC explorations.

Chapter 4, "Anatomy of a Chat Session," walks you through a couple of typical IRC sessions. I show you exactly what appears on your screen as you get on a channel and interact, and I also provide a running commentary to help explain what's going on. This chapter lets you learn by example, and should help put the information from earlier chapters in better perspective.

Chapter 5, "Cyberchat Etiquette," discusses etiquette issues related to chatting on IRC—a few do's and don'ts of Net talk. You wouldn't go to a foreign country without knowing some of its customs and laws first, so why visit the new culture of IRC unprepared?

Chapter 6, "Chat Channels & Related Resources," lists some of the more interesting channels available on IRC. The chapter also discusses other areas of the Net that deal with IRC—such as IRC-related newsgroups, and pages on the World Wide Web.

Finally, the book closes with a reference section, which includes an alphabetical directory of channels, a list of servers for accessing IRC, a glossary, a brief collection of related reading material, and (like all good books) an index.

Well, what are you waiting for? Get out of this introduction and head for Chapter 1! One last tip before we take off: Get a really comfy chair, because many IRCers find Internet Relay Chat quite addicting! Don't say I didn't warn you...

Donald Rose
ac678@lafn.org

THE ABC'S OF IRC

Just what is this thing called IRC? Hmmm... Remember CB radio? Citizen's Band? (Extra points if you also remember the song "Convoy," all the Smokey films and the CB-craze lingo. Ten-four, good buddy.) CB may have been a '70s fad, but it still is a mode of communication that lets anyone with CB access join in a sort of radio free-for-all. Well, Internet Relay Chat, or IRC, is like a kind of text-based CB that operates over the Internet instead of radio waves.

Here's another popular analogy used to visualize and think about IRC: Picture yourself at a large party with people from all over the world, standing around in groups having conversations that you can join in or eavesdrop on at will. You can walk from group to group, and even invite one or more people into a separate room to have a private conversation. And if necessary, you can talk to someone secretly so that no one else can hear.

IRC is a multiuser, multichannel chat system; anyone with IRC access can join in on one or more channels. On any particular day, channels typically number in the hundreds, sometimes even thousands. Each channel is a virtual place, a kind of "Netspace" or, for you Gibson fans, "cyberspace." Each usually has a definite topic of conversation, and can involve groups of people from two to scores, depending on the popularity or the breadth of the topic, or any number of other factors. Unlike other Internet facilities such as e-mail and newsgroups, IRC communication occurs in real time, a feature once considered the sole dominion of oral communication (and visual, if you count the more advanced and expensive video communication systems).

To connect to the IRC network, the IRC user (you!) runs a "client" program. When you type something on your computer while connected to IRC, a "server" program instantly echoes your typed words—that is, your inputs—to all users around the globe who happen to be on the same channel with you. As various people join in with their inputs, one or more conversations result. See Figure 1-1 for a preview of what a typical IRC dialogue looks like.

```
<bird> welcome donrose!
<Heloise> I know who Gypsy is. She lives in Arizona
<Baldric> bird: it's really nice country out there ( bit dry at the moment tho' )
<jaay> wish I were travelling to melbourne though!
> thanks! where is everyone "calling" from?
<bird> where ya from donrose?
<Heloise> jaay, good luck. Where from and where to?
> I am from L.A.
bird is in New Mexico USA
<Heloise> jaay, jump in a car, train or plain, and come
<jaay> hel: sydne (randick) to sydney (litbay)
<Baldric> <----- Melbourne, Oz
<bird> donrose; we have a few regulars there, just a few...
<Heloise> jaay, I know what Ranwick is ( one big race course) but what is the
other place?
*** vulcan [vulcan@ix-sea2-05.ix.netcom.com] has joined #30plus
<Baldric> vulcan, hello
<jaay> helen: typo - little bay
<Heloise> vulcan, hi
<vulcan> Hi, all! :)
<Heloise> jaay, ok, help me more.. which little bay?
```

Figure 1-1: *A brief excerpt from a typical IRC chat session.*

The input area of an IRC client typically consists of a one-line window or section at the bottom of the screen where you type your commands and/or text. Your input, along with the text being typed by the other members of the channel you're on, appears above the input area and scrolls up as new lines appear. This enables you to watch and participate in the conversation. Most IRC clients for home computers (PCs and Macs) even let you save your IRC sessions—either to a scroll buffer (so past discussions can be accessed by "scrolling back in time" as far as the buffer allows) or to a file on disk.

You can join and send your input to existing public group chats—or, unlike CB, you can create your *own* channels (try doing that on radio

Chat Forums on Other Online Services   IRC is not the only virtual chatspace you can access today. For example, America Online, Prodigy, GEnie, Delphi and CompuServe all have similar chat areas for their subscribers to talk on. Due to space limits we cannot specifically cover these non-Internet chat services in this book. However, many of the general principles and ideas (such as those presented in Chapter 5, "Cyberchat Etiquette") can be applied to any chatspace, so if you *are* engaging in online chat on commercial services, feel free to buy this book!

Note that each of these non-IRC chat services is basically an island unto itself; forum chatters on one service cannot talk real-time with those on another (at least that is the standard as of this writing). Even if two forums have the same name and same regular users, someone on service X cannot converse with someone on service Y. However, some services (e.g., Delphi) have begun allowing access to IRC, and there is talk of more online services connecting to IRC in various ways. Hence, IRC may one day become a bridge connecting all the major online commercial services *and* the many millions of Internet users. If and when this occurs, IRC would certainly become (if it isn't already) the largest online chatterverse in the world.

without the FCC coming after you!). Channels can also "die"—disappear from lack of use; if no one's on a channel, it ceases to exist (though it can always be re-created later). You can even create a private channel for yourself and as few as one or two other people. And just like on a CB radio, you can give yourself a unique "handle" or nickname (although on IRC, people rarely seem to type the phrase "good buddy").

The Growth of IRC

IRC developed from "talk," a UNIX program that lets two Net users converse with text via a split screen (one user on top, the other below). This program is still available to most users on UNIX-based systems, but it is generally limited to just a pair of Netters. The ability for three or more users to converse at once came in 1988, when IRC was written by Jarkko Oikarinen (you might still be able to e-mail Jarkko at jto@tolsun.oulu.fi if you want to say thanks). Although designed as a replacement for the "talk" program, it has become much more than that. Since starting in Finland, the system has been used in over 60 countries around the world, and IRC currently links host systems in 20 different countries. IRC is constantly evolving, so the way things work one week may not necessarily be the way they work the next.

IRC gained international fame during two big crises that occurred in 1991. When people could not easily communicate via other means, or were censored, they searched for a solution—and found one in IRC. During the 1991 Persian Gulf War, news updates from around the world came across many networks (the

Internet as well as other media), and many IRC users who were online at the time gathered on a single channel to hear these reports. Unlike other media, IRC was considered to be an uncensored, nearly unbiased source of information. Some of the participants may have been reporting biased news (or news believed to have media-based or government-forced bias) from other sources, but when biased news is broadcast on IRC, people on the channel either label it as such, or quickly come to a mutual understanding that some items are tainted and that others carry more weight. The fast, interactive, multisource nature of IRC makes it a wonderful forum for comparison of information from around the world—so that the "best" information can rise to the top, so to speak—and hence IRC is a perfect arena for understanding, reporting and dealing with crises that are international in scope.

IRC had similar uses during the coup against Mikhail Gorbachev in the summer of 1991, and again during yet another uprising (this time against Gorby successor Boris Yeltsin) in 1993. In both cases, IRC users from Moscow and other areas were giving live reports about the unstable situation there.

But IRC is not well known solely for its use during crises and news storms. IRC has also become a mecca for college students, who often spend hours hanging out in "virtual cafes," chatting on all sorts of subjects. (In fact, some observers and users of the Internet feel that it's the large number of free Internet accounts afforded to college students that leads to the large number of hours spent on IRC.)

People also do commercial work on IRC (it is an excellent forum for consultations between workers on different points of the globe), and a whole range of activities, from programming to translation to collaborative creativity (I even wrote a real-time interactive poem with someone on IRC!) goes on over chat channels.

Still, a large part of IRC activity—the majority, some would argue—is closer to play than work. Since IRC is used by people all over the globe, users of IRC tend to know personally only a few fellow "IRCers." IRC allows, and even encourages, recreational communication between people who never have been, and probably never will be, in a situation where knowledge of one another can be based on physical cues.

IRC was not specifically designed for any single type of environment or social construct (e.g., the business, scientific or educational domain), and ultimately, the way IRC is used is decided by those who use it. Throughout this book we'll be discussing more of the various ways people use and deal with IRC-based communication.

Why IRC Is So Great

You could also call this section "Cool Things You Can Do on IRC." There are many, but here are some highlights to get your mental juices flowing:

- You can talk to your significant other (and, yes, your mom too) for less than the price of a phone call.

- You can experience instant simultaneous news-sharing (e.g., in times of emergency), with worldwide viewpoints and a lower probability of communication censorship than on most other media.

- You can make new friends from all over the world without using up your frequent flyer miles.

- You can discover (or maintain) an affinity with your own (or a different) ethnic group by chatting or getting personal with others who live around the world.

All of the above are things you can do with existing channels that you find on IRC. However, you also can create *new* channels, and eventually you'll want to try it. Why would that be great? Glad you asked:

- You can create a virtual cafe, complete with online poetry readings and instant audience response.

- If you're a scientist, you can converse with colleagues from around the globe for immediate feedback. Or keep up with that student you guided through college, or track down a long-lost professor (who turned out not to be lost but rather busy surfing the Net).

- You can create your own channel for (just about) any topic you want. Even if the topic happens to be "let's get off this over-crowded channel"!

And of course, let's not forget that every activity listed in this section is *free*! Pretty much, that is. "Free," as in completely zero-cost, assumes that your Internet connection is provided at no cost to you. Even if you *do* pay for your connection, your IRC sessions are still close to free, since the flat rate typically charged for Internet access is independent of how many people you chat with online or how many times per month you utilize IRC. As always, "your mileage may vary."

Why IRC Is Not Perfect

What's this? A book on IRC telling you that IRC is not the greatest thing since sliced bread? Don't panic—I just want you to have a well-rounded view of IRC. A good tour guide tells you things to avoid and possible pitfalls as well as the must-see's and must-do's. So here's a sampling of complaints some folks have voiced now and then about IRC, and how to deal with them:

- Some channels may seem like just a bunch of noise, or worse. Yes, it's often true. But you must keep reminding yourself, "alas, such is the nature of democracy"—which should make you feel better for a while. And don't forget, your glorious presence on such channels might increase the signal-to-noise ratio, right?

- There are so many channels to wade through to find the one you want! But luckily you have this book to help alleviate this problem. And besides, variety is the spice of life. What would you prefer, a single IRC shopping channel?

- Some channels have regulars or operators (or both) who are very cliquish, and who may want to keep only certain types of people on their channel—or even just certain individuals, if they decide their channel should be a kind of private (virtual) club. This does happen at times—but you should ask whether it's valuable or enjoyable to go where you are not appreciated. There are so many other channels to venture onto that your creative chat options will remain wide open for a long time. Besides, you can always open your *own* channel. Maybe one day IRC citizens will try to force some "private" channel to open up and stop "discriminating" against fellow IRCers—but for now the IRC (and the Internet in general) is way too anarchistic and libertarian for that to happen.

- IRC can become addictive, and there are many who admit to having succumbed to such a state. But thankfully, methods to deal with IRC addiction have also developed. (For example, see the alt.irc.recovery newsgroup, discussed in Chapter 6.) Is IRC, as some have maintained, just as bad a habit as TV? You, dear reader, will have to decide for yourself—but at least this book will help you recognize the relevant road signs along the IRC information highway (you knew I had to squeeze that metaphor in somewhere).

Life on IRC: What to Expect

Those who have used a CB, or other chat rooms on other services, have a strong head start for understanding life on IRC. If you haven't used any online chat before, or you're rusty on '70s fads, here are some basic tips, hints and assorted expectations related to IRC culture and protocol.

On IRC, you can talk to one person (the minimum human interaction), or you can join a channel populated with scores and scores of folks. (Actually, it is even possible for you to be the only "live person" talking on a channel—see the "Bots" section in Chapter 3.)

Unlike most folks at a real (physical) party, people on IRC can keep track of multiple conversations while on a channel. Whereas in real life you cannot listen to someone without essentially shutting out others to maintain focus, on IRC the talking is "recorded" in text; hence you can follow many dialogue "threads" as the text appears on your screen. You can help your memory even further by capturing the dialogues into a log file (a kind of long-term memory), or you can just use your scrollable buffer (a kind of short-term memory).

Some IRC gurus even dare to join several channels at a time and follow many threads of talk all at once (even on one screen). This is definitely not recommended for new IRC users, because it can get confusing remembering which folks are on which channels, among other things.

Learning to carry on parallel conversations can be tough, especially at first. And if there are a lot of people on a popular channel, it can be hard to keep a conversation going if you're a newcomer to IRC (an IRC "newbie"). Have you ever tried to talk to 70—or even just 20—people in a room at once? Unless you're giving a lecture, probably not. Conversations usually tend to involve around 2 to 7 people on average. Same thing online. So expect to focus on only a few people if a channel is crowded. Then, once you've picked out your 2 to 7 Netters (your optimal range may vary) to focus on, you've got to keep an eye out for their responses (labeled by their names, thank God!)—no small task on a crowded channel with lots of overlapping dialogue.

Also bear in mind that a "lag" time between one user's input (e.g., a question) and someone's reply to that input can often occur, and to varying degrees. There are many causes for this problem. Sometimes lags occur because the network or your service provider is overworked and slower than normal; due to this, your input might appear later on others' screens than on yours. Other times it is because some folks are following multiple channels and aren't focusing exclusively on you or your channel. If *both* of these apply, the lag in getting replies to your inputs can become confusing or annoying. And if others on the channel also happen to be rude or forgetful, this can make matters even worse (but don't blame IRC for that—bad manners happen in real life too).

If you are new on IRC and don't quite have all the commands down yet, you also might get kidded a bit by the other "channelers," but that should be the worst of it—unless you do something *really* bad, in which case you might get flamed. However, once you read the advice in Chapter 5, "Cyberchat Etiquette," that of course should never happen, and soon you'll feel right at home in the IRC environment.

Chat Psychology 101

Can the nature of communication within a kind of text-based virtual world change how we interact with others? In most cases, the answer is yes, and it is useful to know how before jumping blindly into the IRC world.

The first thing you'll want to be aware of is that the anonymity of interaction in environments like IRC allows users to play games with their identities. Following are a few of the types of behavior some IRC users may engage in:

- Experimenting with being different people—which can include doing things that on some level one doesn't want to do, yet feels one must in order to make a fake persona/character consistent and believable.

- Experimenting with different characters in order to see how other people react, then "trying on" the good parts of the characters that provoke a favorable response while avoiding the others.

- Forgetting, ignoring, removing or rising above the "normal" perceived confines of gender, race, age and other "societal conceptions."

In general, IRC-based communication is less bound by conventions than is face-to-face (FTF or F2F) interaction. Anonymity and the physical impression that one is alone can lead many users of IRC to behave in more uninhibited and nonconformist ways than they would in face-to-face encounters. With little regulating feedback to govern behavior, users may act in ways that would not generally be acceptable with people who effectively are total strangers. This can have both positive and negative effects.

For example, some IRCers are shy by nature, and normally wouldn't talk about certain topics with others face to face. But the perceived safety of anonymity can make one feel less self-conscious, and thus willing to engage in more intimate interactions than one might in the real world. In other words, intimacy can tend to blossom more readily in online virtual realms like IRC, between people who might not otherwise have had, or allowed themselves, the chance to become close.

Virtual Sex Change   Thanks to modern technology, it is now possible for someone on IRC to become a virtual sex object simply by pretending to be female. Since real names (first or last) usually are not incorporated into one's IRC nickname, gender information is often missing. Thus changing sex is as simple as changing one's nickname to something that suggests the opposite of one's actual sex. How do users of IRC typically feel or react while posing under an assumed sexual identity? Some female IRCers have stated that they don't like being male because they miss the flattery that women often get online. Other women say they don't feel comfortable having to give more attention than they receive (since females tend to get more attention online). Many other women on the Internet complain about being objectified or harassed more often online than in real life, and males who pose as women on IRC often experience this for the first time.

Personal relationships among participants in online communication systems can often be deep and highly emotional. Some participants in IRC may even come to feel that their best friends are members of their electronic clique or club, even though they rarely see or even meet them "for real." People even carry out on long-distance romantic relationships over IRC—some even get married, and have actually done so over IRC!

On the negative side, however, this same sense of anonymity can also encourage "flaming," and other examples of poor online manners. Flaming is a phenomenon that often includes overly aggressive hostile remarks and other bits of strong language with opinionated and/or personally insulting overtones. Many IRC users will flame people much more readily than they would deliberately insult or offend someone in real life, since anonymity can lead to a feeling of less responsibility for actions—as well as a feeling that "they can't do anything to retaliate since I'm sitting here all alone, detached and anonymous" (if I may exaggerate a bit to make my point).

Despite the occasional tendency of some to become less amiable online, many users of IRC form strong friendships. Part of this phenomenon is due to the common bond of seeking out and exploring a new medium together—a kind of mutual virtual pioneer spirit, fostered by the lure of the "Information Gold Rush" and the spread of the "Information Railroad" (not yet a superhighway, in my opinion). But a large part is also due to the absence of typical obstacles we see or imagine in the real world that inhibit a free exchange between people or encourage shyness. In short, you have the freedom to be someone you usually are not in the real world—and perhaps more importantly, to be more yourself than would usually be acceptable.

IRC & the Rest of the Net

IRC has definitely "spilled over" into other areas of Net communication. On USENET, for example, several newsgroups devoted to various aspects of IRC life have been spawned. One of the most widely utilized groups pertaining to IRC is alt.irc, where IRC participants can go to chat about chat. Another is alt.irc.recovery, for those recovering from IRC addiction (yes, it really does happen).

IRC life has spread to the World Wide Web as well. For example, there now are a number of Web pages associated with some of the more popular IRC channels. The existence of such pages, as well as the IRC-related USENET groups, shows both the increased popularity of IRC as well as chatters' needs for more interaction beyond the limitations of IRC channels. Also note that, on IRC, there currently is no way to view pictures of frequent channel visitors—yet this is something that can be (and is) done on IRC-related WWW pages. See Chapter 6, "Choice Channels & Related Resources," for complete listings and descriptions of IRC-related newsgroups and Web pages.

> **MUDs, MOOs & MUCKs**   IRC is similar in many ways to MUDs (Multi-User Dimensions), areas on the Net where a kind of online VR (virtual reality) takes place. MUDs allow real-time interaction based mainly on social role-playing. Like IRC, MUDs are text-based, and involve networked participants who may be from all corners of the globe. Although this book doesn't contain any direct discussion of MUDs or other types of text-based VR (e.g., MOOs and MUCKs), some of the ideas and concepts, such as those covered in Chapter 5, "Cyberchat Etiquette," will be helpful to users of these Netspaces.

The Undernet

Remember that *Star Trek* episode "Mirror Mirror"? The crew of the Enterprise encountered an alternate universe where there existed a mirror Kirk, a mirror Spock and so on—albeit with slightly altered personalities (naturally, given the need for conflict in an hour-long drama).

Well, the Undernet is like an alternate IRC, a mirror universe of alternative chat channels. In fact, some call this "other network" the

Alternet. All the main concepts in the Undernet online universe—commands, channels, servers, etc.—are essentially analogous to those on IRC. The main technical difference is that the Undernet uses a different set of servers than "regular" IRC does. Connecting to an Undernet server gets you a different set of channels to choose from than connecting to an IRC server—though there are often channels with the same name in both "universes."

Also, regulars on the Undernet (at least according to the official Undernet FAQ) are striving to make it a more Netiquette-savvy, less politicized place to interact than IRC has become over the years. In any case, those on the Undernet encourage you to check out their mirror chatspace. At the very least, the lower numbers of people (it hasn't been around as long as IRC, after all) mean that you have more chances for privacy and minimized interruptions (if that's your preference when using Net chat).

Moving On

By now you should have an initial sense of what things you can look forward to doing or seeing on chat channels, what kinds of behavior you might expect to find while chatting, how IRC relates to other areas of the Internet, and other nice bits of information you may never have known before (but will cherish forever). And hopefully, you also have an irresistible urge to read on!

The next couple of chapters will cover the detailed steps involved in actually making an IRC connection, and guide you through your first attempt at getting onto IRC. And of course, there's lots of other stuff to come, too. But don't just take my word for it—turn the page!

GETTING CONNECTED

Now that you know the basics of what IRC is, what it can do, and how it fits into the Net as a whole, it's time to actually get yourself onto the IRC network. In this chapter you'll get a step-by-step guide. First we'll take a look at the various types of Internet connections, and at how the type of connection you have affects the route you must follow to get onto IRC. Next you'll find out how to retrieve and configure an IRC client appropriate for your type of Internet connection, and how to point your client to a valid IRC server. (Those of you who are too impatient to find and configure a real IRC client will learn how to telnet to a public IRC server—you'll also learn why this really should be considered only a temporary alternative.) And finally, you'll find out about connecting to the Undernet, IRC's "little sibling."

Necessary Connections

In order to access IRC, you need to have one of the following types of Internet connection:

- A shell account
- A SLIP/PPP account
- A direct Internet account

It's great to have options, but many of you may be unclear about how to choose among these multiple routes to IRC. The following sections serve as a kind of road map, helping you understand more about these different routes and how to get to your ultimate destination, the chat channels. (If you already have one of these types of Internet accounts and you're happy with it, your choice may be already made, but it won't kill you to know a little bit more about the type of connection you have.)

IRC via Shell Account

With a shell account, you might dial in via modem to an Internet service provider, such as Netcom or Delphi, and use their client programs (running on their machines) which are already set up to give you easy access to IRC. This route is often the cheapest, because when IRC access is available, it's usually included in the flat rate many pay for shell accounts.

Updated Service Provider Lists Updated periodically, the Nixpub list is a widely used source for Internet service providers. You can look for the current version via anonymous FTP at rtfm.mit.edu in the pub/usenet-by-group/alt.bbs directory. You can also search the various Net-related newsgroups on USENET, where the Nixpub list is sometimes posted. If you don't yet have access to the Internet, you can always ask someone you know who *is* connected to get it and snail-mail you a hardcopy. (Of course, by the time you get it, you'll probably be connected!)

If you use a shell account, you might not have to worry about most of the information provided in the rest of this chapter. Getting onto IRC for you can be as easy as typing **irc** from the prompt of an appropriate menu or window on the shell service. This is often the case on UNIX-based Internet providers, so give it a try.

If a simple "irc" command or something similar does *not* work, then you probably need to get an IRC client (designed for UNIX, if your shell account is with a UNIX-based Internet provider; since UNIX is the most common operating system used on Net-connected machines, this is a good bet). In this case, this chapter *is* still important, so keep reading.

Note that while having a client already "built in" to your account is convenient—requiring little or no setup time from the user, and little or no direct interaction with the client—these semi-invisible shell-account clients are often less adaptable to your needs (e.g., you may be stuck with only one client when there are newer, better ones becoming available, and you may have no options to customize the client you must use). It's kind of like automatic versus manual transmission in a car; auto is easier to use, but with manual you can always change to the exact gear you want.

IRC via SLIP/PPP Account

With a SLIP (Serial Line Internet Protocol) or PPP (Point-to-Point Protocol) account, you dial into an Internet service provider and establish a temporary, direct connection to the Internet, which usually gives you faster performance than a shell account. In order to use a SLIP/PPP account, you must obtain and configure SLIP/PPP connection software. If you're using a Mac, you'll also need MacTCP (the latest version of this program is often available on the Net and/or from Apple). And if you're a Windows user, you'll need to get Win-Sock (the most recent versions of programs that use WinSock are available at ftp.cica.indiana.edu and other FTP sites as well).

To access IRC using your SLIP/PPP account, you must find and download an IRC client, set up the client for proper use on your computer, point the client to the right server, and finally make the connection to the IRC server by running your client. (We'll look at these steps in detail later in this chapter.)

If all this software searching, fiddling and running seems too involved for you, you might be happier with a shell account, which may

SLIP/PPP Access Is Easier Than Ever Getting a SLIP/PPP Internet connection is now easier and more affordable than ever. While still more costly on average than most shell accounts, the rates for the speedier and more comprehensive SLIP/PPP connections have been plummeting. If you don't already have SLIP/PPP access, detailed advice on the necessary software components is readily available in convenient book/disk combinations such as the *Internet Membership Kit* (from Ventana Media), *The Windows Internet Tour Guide* or *The Mac Internet Tour Guide* (both from Ventana Press). These packages provide all the useful or required programs and the information you need to set them up properly, as well as special access offers from commercial Internet service providers.

be slower but probably involves less work in the short run. But for many users, the greater flexibility and level of Internet access offered by a SLIP/PPP connection may be worth the extra effort.

IRC via Direct Connection

A direct (or "dedicated") Internet connection is often provided to those who are using computers at businesses, government offices and universities—especially the bigger institutions. A direct connection requires TCP/IP software, which allows your computer to communicate with other computers on the Internet, but you shouldn't have to worry about it; your system (network) administrator should install and configure it for you. To connect to IRC, you'll also need a client appropriate for you computer.

Note that if you work at a site that has a local network running TCP/IP but no connection to the Internet, you cannot use IRC. If your site has an Internet connection but no IRC server on the local network, you will need to connect to a server outside it—but many sites explicitly inhibit non-local connections for certain machines. On machines that are open to the public—for example, in university computing centers—people have been known to abuse network access by FTPing large amounts of data from all corners of the earth. Restricting network access is considered the only way of dealing with this problem. If this is the case, politely ask your system administrator to lift that restriction (and in general, seek out this "sysadmin" if you want to clear up any questions about direct connections).

Some sites are still hesitant about allowing IRC use, for fear that it may put too much load on the network. Since this is usually not the case, you can try to open up restricted access to IRC by contacting the powers that be and using reasonable, well-planned arguments. And perhaps this book.

Getting an IRC Client

Whatever method you use to access IRC, you almost always need an IRC client (see the "Telnet" section later in this chapter for an exception). Just what does a client actually do? It handles the dirty work for you, reaching out over the Net to find the server you want (or, in some cases, searching for others if your default choice is unavailable) and making the connection with that server. Think of the client as you sticking your arm out, and the server as another arm coming out to shake your hand. If the shake goes well (as it usually does), you're transported onto IRC. Quite a nifty bit of coding, these clients.

Some users already have a client installed on the system they are using; for example, many shell Internet accounts use UNIX and hence UNIX-based clients. For shell users, accessing IRC can be as easy as typing **irc**. However, if you have a SLIP/PPP account or a direct Internet connection, you'll need to get a client designed for your platform in order to access and use IRC.

If you don't have a client already, you can download one from the Net. You can get clients via anonymous FTP from any of the sites listed (in general, it is best to use the site closest to you). If you don't know what anonymous FTP is, ask your local guru (e.g., a system administrator or operator person at your service provider) to show you, or get onto the Net and read the FAQ about anonymous FTP. (In fact, this advice about FAQs goes for almost any question you may have about life online). Following are some of the sites you should search for IRC clients, broken down by the platform/operating system you're using.

Macintosh

Right now, the ircle client is probably the most popular IRC software for the Macintosh. The Homer client has garnered more and more attention lately, however, in part because of its companion program HomerPaint, which enables Netters to create collaborative art over IRC. (Painting instead of talking! Maybe now we can finally test whether a picture really is worth a thousand words.) Homer offers a lot of other nice features, too. User-friendly windows and buttons replace the standard IRC typed "slashline" commands; sound effects indicate channel navigation; text from other IRCers can be spoken in fairly distinct artificially-produced voices (requires Apple's Speech Manager software—try ftp.apple.com to get it); the TCP version (running over SLIP or PPP connections) allows DCC (Direct Client Connection) file transfers so you and others on a channel can exchange batches of information. Not bad for $25 shareware! (System 7 or later and a minimum of 4mb of RAM are recommended to use Homer.)

You can look for the ircle and Homer clients (as well as other useful Mac software) at the following sites:

Site Name	Directory Path
zaphod.ee.pitt.edu	/pub
sumex-aim.stanford.edu	/info-mac/comm
ftp.funet.fi	/pub/Unix/irc/mac
ftp.ira.uka.de	/pub/systems/mac
cs-ftp.bu.edu	/irc/clients/macintosh
cs.bu.edu	/irc/clients/macintosh
mac.archive.umich.edu	/mac/util/comm

Another client you can use on the Mac is ircII, but this client is used more often on UNIX systems (see the "UNIX" section below).

Microsoft Windows

Windows types will probably want to find the client called winirc (I say "probably" because the ongoing spread of both Windows and IRC means there may be other Windows clients available by the time you read this). Look for winirc at cs-ftp.bu.edu in the /irc/clients/pc/windows directory (or try the /irc/clients/msdos directory).

You can also use the ircII client with Windows, but again, this client is used more often on UNIX systems.

MS-DOS

The following locations should reveal several potential IRC clients for DOS users. Look at ftp.funet.fi in the /pub/Unix/irc/msdos directory. Also check out cs-ftp.bu.edu in the /irc/clients/pc/msdos directory (or try the /irc/clients/msdos directory).

UNIX

The most popular UNIX client for IRC is ircII. If you're using a shell account on a UNIX-based computer, this client may already be installed (see earlier discussion). If not, try searching the /irc/clients directory at cs.bu.edu (or cs-ftp.bu.edu). The ircII software as well as compilation instructions for UNIX should be there. The software files will probably be named ircII2.2.9.tar.Z and ircII2.2.9help.tar.Z, or something similar. (Note: The file names might end in slightly different letters, such as *gz* instead of *Z*; get the files whose suffixes you recognize and that you're confident you can uncompress on your end using compression utility programs that you have. See the "Unpacking Your Client" section below for more on compression and other types of file manipulations).

Platforms, Shmatforms Although some of the examples and illustrations in this book use the Macintosh platform, don't fret if you don't use a Mac. The type of platform you use really doesn't matter much once you're on IRC—which, after all, mainly involves text writing within a window. More important than platform considerations is the way in which you ponder/invent/read/interpret/answer that text—*that* is the heart and magic of IRC!

If you don't know how to install UNIX-based clients, or don't want to know, or simply like any kind of automation, then you can try using a completely automatic IRC client installer. Provided you have 1.5mb or more of space on your disk (on whatever UNIX machine you're using), or have at least that much room allocated to your account, you can try issuing the following command:

telnet sci.dixie.edu 1 | sh

The result should be an attempt to auto-install. (No warranty here, however; you might want to get advice from UNIX gurus or other experts at your Net service provider before trying this.)

Following are some other FTP sites that may have UNIX-based IRC clients to download:

Site Name	Directory Path
ftp.acsu.buffalo.edu	/pub/irc
ftp.funet.fi	/pub/Unix/irc
coombs.anu.edu.au	/pub/irc
slopoke.mlb.semi.harris.com	/pub/irc
ftp.informatik.tu-muenchen.de	/pub/comp/networking/irc/clients

A tip that may help you UNIX users: If you know where the symbolic link CURRENT is, find out which file this link points to; CURRENT should be linked to the most recent UNIX source code for the ircII client.

Other Platforms

Following are locations where you can access clients for operating systems that are currently less "hot" (usage-wise) than Mac, Windows, DOS and UNIX:

Emacs

For the diehard Emacs fans out there (and they are a dedicated group), there are at least two ELISP clients for Emacs: Kiwi and IRChat. But the usual advice is to use ircII rather than spend time installing these clients, unless you are fluent in Emacs. If you must go the Emacs route, here are some locations to peruse for clients and information:

Site Name	Directory Path
cs-ftp.bu.edu	/irc/clients/elisp
cs.hut.fi	/pub/irchat
slopoke.mlb.semi.harris.com	/pub/irc/emacs
ftp.funet.fi	/pub/Unix/irc/Emacs
ftp.informatik.tu-muenchen.de	/pub/comp/networking/irc/clients

OS/2

For clients that run under the OS/2 operating system (for PCs), take a look at cs-ftp.bu.edu in the /irc/clients/pc/os2 directory. Also try hobbes.nmsu.edu in the /os2/2_x/network directory.

X11

For X11 clients, take a look at catless.ncl.ac.uk in the /pub directory, and harbor.ecn.purdue.edu in the /pub/tcl/code directory.

VMS

Try these sites for clients used under the VMS operating system:

Site Name	Directory Path
cs-ftp.bu.edu	/irc/clients/vms
coombs.anu.edu.au	/pub/irc/vms
ftp.funet.fi	/pub/Unix/irc/vms
ftp.informatik.tu-muenchen.de	/pub/net/irc

VM

Finally, here are some locations to look at to find REXX, the client you need if you use VM:

Site Name	Directory Path
cs-ftp.bu.edu	/irc/clients/rxirc
ftp.informatik.tu-muenchen.de	/pub/net/irc/VM
coombs.anu.edu.au	/pub/irc/rxirc
ftp.funet.fi	/pub/Unix/irc/rxirc
ftp.informatik.uni-oldenburg.de	/pub/irc/rxirc

Unpacking Your Client

Using the info above, you now have downloaded your client application. But programs that you download from the Net are usually *compressed* (to save storage space as well as download time required), and they might also be *encrypted* (for privacy/protection reasons) or manipulated in other ways. For each form of manipulation, you'll need the proper program to "unmanipulate" the client before you can use it.

There are usually just a few main types of manipulations used on IRC clients or other files. These typically involve BinHex, Zip, Tar or one of several popular personal computer compression utilities (StuffIt is the most popular and well known of the compression programs; another is CompactPro). You can quickly spot files that have been manipulated by such software once you get used to the file extensions associated with the various programs and utilities. Here's a handy table to help guide you:

Extension	Compression Program/Utility Used
hqx	BinHex
zip	Zip
sit	StuffIt
cpt	CompactPro
tar	Tar (a UNIX compression command)
Z	compress (another UNIX compression command)

In most cases, before you can use a downloaded client or other file, you must uncompress the file (e.g., UnStuff a .sit file using StuffIt), and then undo any other encodings (e.g., UnZip a Zipped file). Most of the popular file manipulation programs can be downloaded from the Net. Some variant of StuffIt (e.g., StuffIt Deluxe, version 3.0.2) is a well-accepted standard for compression as well as uncompression. This software is also convenient because it can undo other manipulations (since it has "translators" for UnZipping, Untarring, encoding/decoding BinHexed files, and so on). Most of the major computer platforms (such as Mac and Windows) use similar procedures for manipulating and unmanipulating files.

Configuring Your Client

Now that you have a client in runnable form, you'll probably need to configure it. Like most programs, the clients have default settings that you can try to get away with using, but it's best to check the current configuration and adjust as needed to optimize the client for the system you are going to run it on. Follow the instructions that are available for the client you choose; usually you can access documentation files for your client in the same directory where you found the client.

Most configuration procedures involve choosing the right server—the site that runs IRC and gives your client access to it. In the next section we'll discuss the details of that sometimes tricky selection process.

The Receiving End: Choosing a Server

The client alone cannot get you onto IRC; you need to find a server to help you complete the connection. (The saying "it takes two to tango" applies even to the Internet!) The IRC network consists of a number of interconnected servers all over the world, and clients that can connect to these servers. To use IRC you have to know the address (hostname or IP number) of a server that you can use.

If you are using the Internet within an organization, an easy way to find a server is to watch the screen when a colleague who is already set up to use IRC initiates a connection. The server will give its name with a welcome message that should resemble the following:

```
*** Your host is server-name [host.name], running version xxxx.
```

If you are in a large organization, you might even have your own server, or a preferred server that most everyone uses. If you use a commercial service provider that has knowledgeable Netizens or IRCers at your disposal, you can ask them to recommend a good server address for you to use.

If you try these suggestions and you still can't find the right server to use, try one of the servers from the list below. Due to the fast-paced change that is the nature of the Net these days, some of these sites could possibly be gone or unavailable by the time you read this book, or some may have changed names. (As a general rule, the bigger the site, the more likely that it will remain stable over time.) Also keep in mind that the following list is not comprehensive. Nevertheless, it is a good beginning; one of the servers below should be fine for most readers.

Server Address	Geographical Location
irc.math.ufl.edu	Florida
irc.uiuc.edu	Illinois
copper.ucs.indiana.edu	Indiana
cs-pub.bu.edu	Boston
csa.bu.edu	Boston
irc.colorado.edu*	Colorado
olymp.wu-wien.ac.at 6666	Austria
irc.funet.fi	Finland
cismhp.univ-lyon1.fr	France
disuns2.epfl.ch	Europe
irc.nada.kth.se	Europe
sokrates.informatik.uni-kl.de	Europe
bim.itc.univie.ac.at	Europe
ircserver.cltr.uq.oz.au	Australia
jello.qabc.uq.oz.au	Australia

* Try port 6665 or 6666 if 6667 gives trouble.

An initial rule of thumb for choosing servers is to use the server that can be reached from your site at minimum delay and network load—this usually means the geographically closest site. You can always ask about which is the best server for you when you get on IRC, on a help-oriented channel such as #irchelp (see Chapter 6 for more on specific channels). You can also ask about this on one of the USENET newsgroups that usually handle new users' questions pertaining to IRC (alt.irc, alt.irc.questions or news.answers).

Note that not all servers allow all clients in. When you get a message about being rejected by the server, find another server. All servers are part of the same network and have the same information, persons and channels.

Port Numbers The port number used by most IRC servers is 6667, but a different number can be entered in case there are special applications such as site-specific local servers that use a different port. Usually you don't have to worry about this, but most server lists provide the required port number if it isn't 6667. Also, some servers state alternate port numbers in their welcome messages.

If the servers you try don't work for some reason, Appendix B lists additional publicly accessible server sites. A complete list of servers also is sometimes posted in the alt.irc newsgroup. And a comprehensive list of active IRC servers is available by anonymous FTP at cs.bu.edu in the /irc/support directory. Access the file entitled servers.*YYXXXX* to get an up-to-date server list (where the *YY* part indicates the current year and the *XXXX* part indicates the month and day this file was last updated). Keep in mind, however, that not all servers listed in this file are publicly accessible. You can also read the IRC FAQ for server information.

In addition, you can always seek out advice from established IRC gurus such as Helen Trillian Rose (one of the best-known IRC experts), who gives IRC advice via her WWW home page. Other folks also maintain useful Web pages, and all of these people are generally reachable via e-mail as well if you have a question (but don't abuse their time with too many queries, especially if such questions are already covered in the various IRC FAQs, primers and tutorials available online).

Making the Connection

Now you have your client (or you know that your system has one built in), you know what server to connect to and that server's proper port number, and you personal computer users have your client configured in a manner optimal for your machine. And naturally, you have something you're dying to say to someone somewhere out there. You're ready to make contact!

If you're using a shell account, to actually make the connection to IRC you probably need only enter the command **irc** at your service's normal input prompt. Ask your service provider for more help if you need it.

If you're using a SLIP/PPP account or a direct connection (and therefore are running your client program on your own computer), launch your client. (SLIP/PPP users will be required to launch a SLIP program to make the connection to the Internet before running the IRC client.) The client program then will connect you to your desired IRC server. (Some users will be asked to provide some initial information—usually about the desired server—before the client completes the IRC connection.) Once the client's initial startup actions are finished, you should be connected to IRC.

If you are using a menu-driven client program, such as those that run on a Mac or Windows, a menu bar should be visible; the menus typically contain commands useful for IRC operations. Some clients have built-in help to aid your understanding of the menu commands, or you can try entering **/help** on IRC itself. Or you can be bold and simply experiment with selecting various commands from the menus in order to learn about their operation. Also visible at this stage are one or more windows for reading and entering information to/from IRC channels. The next chapter goes into more detail about all this, so be patient and keep reading!

> **The IRC FAQ** Of course, all good Netters know that whenever they have questions, about servers, clients or anything else, they should look for a FAQ first (remember the old line, "just the FAQs, please"). The IRC FAQ is available many places; for instance, the URL location for World Wide Web access to it is http://www.kei.com/irc.html. The FAQ can also be accessed via anonymous FTP at cs.bu.edu in the /irc/support/alt-irc-faq directory.

Telnet: The "Other" Way to Get Onto IRC

If you truly have no access to IRC servers, or you somehow cannot access the proper client you need, or you just want to try IRC briefly before you get a regular connection using one of the options discussed earlier, you can connect to IRC via telnet, although this is *not* recommended as an optimal long-term solution. Many telnettable IRC server sites limit either the hours you can telnet in, or the number of users, or both. In addition, these sites usually can't handle excess loads, and are often slow and very unreliable. For all these reasons, IRC gurus implore Netters (especially those who are newbies on IRC) to use telnetting-to-IRC as a last resort only. You should truly have a pressing need and absolutely no alternative before taking the telnet route.

If you're using a shell account, you can probably use your service's built-in telnet facility by simply entering the command **telnet**. If your provider does not have telnet *and* doesn't allow IRC, you might want to search for a new service! (Seriously, there are so many providers now, you are bound to find a reasonably-priced one that has at least one of these two functions.)

If you are using a SLIP/PPP account or a direct Internet connection, you can find and use a telnet program designed for your computer. Finding and downloading a telnet program is similar to finding IRC clients. This topic is covered elsewhere in more detail than we have room for here (again, packages such as Ventana's *Internet Membership Kit* and *Internet Tour Guide* books are good sources of information about this and other issues related to making the most of your SLIP/PPP account). However, here's some quick advice for getting a telnet program for your computer: FTP a free public-domain version from the Net. Telnet for Windows and Mac, for example, is usually located in the same location as Mosaic and other commonly used Internet programs, or in a nearby directory. One location many Netters try is the NCSA site (anonymous FTP to ftp.ncsa.uiuc.edu).

Okay—so how do you actually use telnet to get onto IRC? You treat the session like any other telnet session. For example, if using a shell account's built-in telnet capability, you could type the following:

telnet ircclient.itc.univie.ac.at 6668

If you are using NCSA Telnet or another telnet client with a SLIP/PPP account or direct connection, an IRC telnet session is accomplished just like any other (non-IRC) telnet session, except the server you are telnetting to happens to give you access to IRC.

There are a number of servers designed to receive users via telnet. You can try telnetting to the site given in the example above (that is, until you get off your duff and FTP a genuine IRC client from one of the many IRC-related repositories you'll find online!). You can also try telnetting to bradenville.andrew.cmu.edu. Note that the port number is often different than the standard port number (6667) used by most non-telnet IRC servers.

If you need other sites, or prefer telnetting via graphical user interfaces like Mosaic and Netscape, there are some World Wide Web pages that contain links to telnettable IRC servers. For instance, check out the page shown in Figure 2-1; this WWW page contains links to other telnettable IRC sites in the U.S., as well as some in Europe. (Need more info? You can surf to an IRC FAQ via this page as well.)

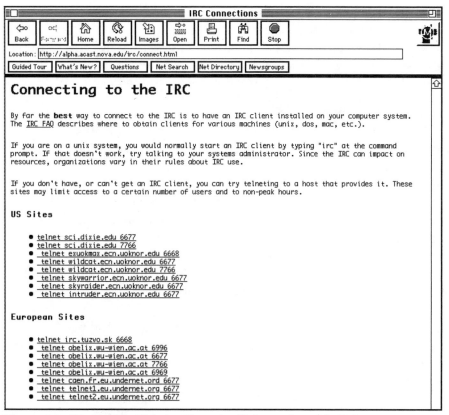

Figure 2-1: *World Wide Web page featuring links to telnettable IRC servers.*

Let's Not Forget the Undernet

Most of the information in this chapter about connecting to IRC also applies to getting onto the Undernet (recall that Undernet is like a mirror IRC, an alternate chat universe). However, the servers you will access are almost certainly going to be different than those providing IRC access. For information on which Undernet servers to use, and all sorts of other useful stuff, you can check out the alt.irc.undernet newsgroup, or read the Undernet FAQ. The FAQ should appear periodically on the Undernet newsgroup. It's also available via anonymous FTP at rtfm.mit.edu in the /pub/usenet-by-group/alt.irc directory. If you just can't wait to find an Undernet server, try sanjose.ca.us.undernet.org (located in San Jose, CA).

You can FTP clients, and probably other Undernet-related goodies, from ftp.undernet.org. For even more info you can also search the IRC-related sites mentioned throughout this book.

Moving On

Now you have the big picture of what IRC is and how it operates in general, plus the details about finding clients and using them to connect to ready-and-willing servers. But you may still feel hesitant and a bit shy about leaping onto IRC at this point, and you might want to read more about IRC to make sure you're prepared. In Chapter 3 we'll take a closer look at some of the key concepts you'll want to be familiar with before you plunge too deeply into IRC, including channels, operators, nicknames and bots, and we'll examine the actual commands you'll use to manipulate and move around in the IRC environment.

IRC COMMANDS & CONCEPTS

Now that you know how to get onto IRC, you have to learn what to do once you're there! In this chapter you'll find out. To start things off, you'll get the lowdown on essential IRC terms and concepts, some of which were touched on briefly in the first two chapters. Before you start IRCing, you'll also need to learn some basic commands, and the main ones you'll need are covered here. Next, you'll learn about the types of client windows you'll be dealing with while using IRC, and about composing, entering and saving your dialogue while you're on a channel. Finally, you'll get some basic advice to help make your first chat explorations easier.

A Deeper Look at Key Concepts

This section provides more details about important terms and ideas mentioned briefly in various parts of the first two chapters, as well as some new ones. These are concepts you should know fairly well before you actually make the leap onto IRC. The facts and tips presented here will help you make sense of the IRC environment and enhance your chatting experience.

Channels

When you connect to an IRC server, you are on a kind of "limbo" space—sometimes referred to or thought of as a "zero," "dead" or "null" channel—and from there you can do a number of the commands discussed in the "Some Useful IRC Commands" section later in this chapter. For example, you can join one of the "real" channels where you actually talk to others and do the real work or have the real fun you want out of IRC. You can even join more than one channel at the same time—we'll see an example of this in the next chapter—but such an experience is something akin to watching multiple TV programs at the same time and hence is best left to advanced IRC explorers.

If IRC were a person, we might call it a multiple personality; it is made up of many different channels, each of which has a unique name and operates in parallel with all the other channels. There are thousands of parallel discussions and games and other sorts of activities, all going on at the same time.

All channel names begin with the # character. If you attempt to join a channel that does not exist, IRC will create the channel for you. At first you will be the only one on the new channel, but you can wait for others to join you; with a compelling title or topic for your channel, this might not take too long! If you are the first person to join the channel, you are its operator (or, as some prefer to think of it, "king" or "lord" or even "god"). As such, you have certain powers over the channel's operations, such as whether it's private or not.

Nicknames

Your nickname (or nick) is analogous to a "handle" on CB radio, or the special label you use within your e-mail address (the part before the @ sign). It serves to set you apart from other users, both literally (everyone must have a unique label so that IRC can route information properly) and figuratively (since one's nick can indicate one's personality). Your nick is the name by which you will be known to other people on IRC; each line of text you send to the network will be prefixed by your nickname on other users' screens.

When you first enter IRC, your nickname by default will most likely be your user ID, but you can change it with the /nick command. For example, to change your nickname to "wiredweenie," you'd enter the following: **/nick wiredweenie.**

If you use UNIX, you can create a special text file in your home directory called .ircrc (don't forget the period) to automatically execute this slick nick quick-change every time you enter IRC. If you do not use UNIX, check around the Internet to learn other ways of automatically selecting a certain nick upon each login to IRC.

You can choose any nickname that you like, as long as it's constructed from printable characters without any spaces, and no longer than nine characters. (Look at other nicks to get a rough idea of typical lengths and other characteristics.) Plus, be cognizant of the fact that no two people on the network can use the same nick at one time (kind of like an online version of the physics principle that prevents two identical objects from occupying the same space at the same time—remember that climactic scene in *TimeCop*?). Prepare to be presented with an error message if a collision occurs; in such a case, you probably will not be able to proceed until you've chosen another nickname.

The Late, Great NickServ NickServ was a nickname registration service based in Germany that held the nicknames of regular IRC users in a database and would inform you if you had chosen a nick that had been registered by some other user. NickServ went down in the spring of 1994, and some say it will never be back; perhaps it will by the time you read this. Either way, one should still always make an effort to avoid using nicks that others are already employing. Nicknames are not owned, but it is considered bad manners to use some other user's nick.

System Messages

From time to time, systems messages—lines of text that are informative as opposed to part of any ongoing conversations—may appear on a channel. Lines that begin with three asterisks show system messages, such as the following:

```
*** Leather [heather@someplace.com] has joined #metalhead
```

This message says that the user nicknamed Leather, logging in from the address heather@someplace.com, just joined the #metal channel.

Channel Operators

Also known as "chanops," "operators," or just "ops," these are the IRC users "in charge" of a channel. The first person to join a channel (i.e., its creator) automatically gets channel operator status, and can either "rule" alone or share ruling status with anyone he or she wants. Hence, there may be one or more ops on a channel that already exists. The person who founded the channel is typically one of the ops, but this is not always so.

The op (or ops) usually have the power to kick people off the channel for any number of reasons, ranging from those that seem to make sense to those that smack of weirdness—but such is the nature of democracy, remember? If you don't like this, you can always start your own channel and become a channel operator there.

An operator can be spotted online by the @ symbol next to his/her nickname in the list generated by a /names command, or an @ next to the channel name in the output of a /whois command. (See descriptions of these commands later in this chapter.)

IRC Operators

These people maintain the IRC network. They cannot fix channel problems, they cannot kick someone out of a channel for you, and they cannot temporarily kick someone out of IRC for you—hence many users don't bother thinking much about these of ops. But it can't hurt to know about their existence, just in case you ever meet any—they might get impatient with you if you mistake them for the channel op variety.

Bots

A shorthand term, describing online software "robots." Typically they operate from a program or script that is designed to either generate dialogue, or recognize it, or both (having both capabilities is generally a minimum requirement for a bot to seem reasonably human-like and/or intelligent—stop me before this spawns another book!). Bots are generally not needed for IRC chatting to run smoothly, and many servers even ban them. But the concept still comes up often on various channels, so be aware of them.

When they are not blindly banned, bots often serve as automated knowledge dispensers, responding to user requests by providing information or files. They can also be used to keep a channel active automatically, since a channel disappears if no beings (human or bot) are joined to it. This can be useful if an operator wants to keep a channel continuously available, rather than having to recreate it constantly. Other channels may use bots to help run online games that take place on those channels. For instance, the #RiskyBus channel uses a "RobBot" to help run the game—handling the administration of questions and answers, recognizing when players have responded, and so forth. Programmed in this type of benign, no-bad-intentions way, bots can be a positive thing.

As mentioned above, many servers (especially in the U.S.) have started to ban *all* bots, and some server administrators are adamant about keeping bots out of their system (no "bots" about it, if you will). This is because bots can also be disruptive, such as when some Netter programs one to spew out lines like a virtual Valdez, spilling verbal sludge into the sea of IRC chat. Other servers do allow bots, but suggest that they be used sparingly. Some ban bots with such fervor that if you run a bot on their server, you will be banned from using that server. Fortunately, servers generally warn users as they log in by posting a large "NO BOTS!" message in the initial welcome screen, so if you want to stay out of trouble you usually can.

Lag Time

Don't confuse this with athletes' "hang time"—although both *do* involve a delayed action of sorts.

Often you will see IRCers refer to a user, or even an entire channel, as being "lagged"; I have even had some folks tell me that I was *"way lagged."* Being lagged means that there is a delay between the time you send your inputs (by pressing Enter or Return) and the time everyone on the channel can see them. This condition is not good for anyone on a channel (since consecutive delayed appearances of text can seem like random annoying noise), but it is probably worst for the lagged person. Why? Because this person (a) may not even know he or she is lagged, and (b) may have to endure much wrath from other IRCers if his or her inputs keep popping up in weird places, often without any immediate explanation.

There is no foolproof way to guard against being lagged; use /help or consult the help channels on IRC to find out more about this phenomenon. Some initial things to try if you learn that you're lagged include using another IRC server or another client program, or getting onto IRC at another time of day, when servers and channels are less busy.

Some Useful IRC Commands

Now we're getting into specific things you can do on IRC. When you input a command, the IRC server responds in a certain way. Action, reaction. Other than the dialogue text you'll input when you're on a channel, commands will be your primary inputs—your main tools for manipulating and understanding your IRC environment.

When you type a command directly to IRC (i.e., in the proper input area), it must begin with a "/" symbol (note the direction of the slash), which tells IRC that the rest of the line is not something you're saying on a channel but rather some answer or action you want the system to provide or do.

Note that if you get a message stating that your command was not recognized, it could be a misspelling—but it could also be a case of accidentally starting what you intended to be a sentence of dialogue with the "/" symbol. Hey, it happens. So remember to be careful your first few sessions, when things are newest and your brain and hands are on overdrive.

The following subset of IRC commands, while not exhaustive, should serve you well for a large portion of your needs, especially during the beginning stages of your cyberchat life.

Note: When I state something in <brackets> below, it is describing not literal text, but rather what *kind* of information should be used for that part of the command (often one of the command arguments). For example, <channel-name> means that you would type in the actual name of a channel (without the brackets), not the string "<channel-name>."

/help

Gives you a list of useful commands and/or helpful information; a great "last resort" if IRC has you confused or you're just not sure what to do next. For some clients (like ircle, the one I use), issuing this command cause a help window to pop onto your screen; you can keep it open for easy access or close it whenever you want.

/help <command>

Gives you helpful information about a command. For example, **/help list** gives you information about the /list command. You can also try the command **/help intro** followed by **/help newuser** to access help information designed for new users.

/nick <new-nickname>

Changes your nickname—the name by which other IRCers see and refer to you—to anything you'd like (but remember that nine characters is the maximum nick length). For example, **/nick cooldood** changes your nickname to "cooldood." IRCers can use the /whois command to find out your e-mail address (which, unlike your nickname, cannot normally change from session to session). If you try to join a channel where someone else is already using the nickname you wanted to use, IRC may ask you to select another name.

/list

Lists every active/current channel (i.e., channels that currently have IRCers on it), plus the topic of each channel (assuming a topic even exists—sometimes there are none).

    The /list command, when used without arguments, may be a good way to discover what channels are out there (especially for beginners), but it is usually too long for most people to use often (especially non-beginners, who naturally quest for shortcuts and time savings). Since the response to this command can be a very long list, with channels often numbering in the thousands, the following variants of the command are often more useful.

/list -min <thismany>

Lists all channels that are inhabited by at least <thismany> users (the argument <thismany> being a number); for example, **/list -min 10** only lists channels with 10 or more IRCers. Using this method, your list will only display information on the most popular channels (where one can effectively define "popular" by the choice of numeric argument).

An example of this use of /list with a "min" argument is shown in Figure 3-1. Each line lists a channel name, the number of users on that channel at the time the command was given, and that channel's current topic. Note that the topic is basically a message and not always meant to be very informative, nor is it always indicative of the channel's content. In fact, many are quite tongue-in-cheek, or designed as jokes meant mainly for regular visitors. One more (timesaving) tip: If you don't understand the language used in the topic, it's a good bet you won't understand the channel's dialogue either!

```
    Channel User   Name
   #AmigaGer  27
#$B6e=#;38}   20   $B$/$=$h$P$o$j!*$J$s$F$d$D$@!*$R$,$7$O!*(B
#$B$A$c$C$H   64
   #germany   20   the friendly german channel (TM)
        #42   38   Noop on pihtari.
   #freenet   26
   #espana    28   Ultimo dia de los Industriales en el IRC!!!!
     #os/2    20   Come here to talk about OS/2 !
     #root    26
   #WARUNG    23   SALAM PERKENALAN
    #chaos    22
    #amiga    37   He's gone now.  Let's talk about him.....
   #POLSKA    36   Ach ta nasza telekomunikacja!!!!
    #seoul    21   No Duh
```

Figure 3-1: *Partial output resulting from the command* /list -min 20.

/list <channel-name>

Lists information about a specific channel; for instance, /list #sex gives info about the #sex channel only. If you are not sure of the name of the channel you're interested in, you can do a search on part of the likely name, using wildcards. For instance, /list *sex* lists and gives information on all channels with names that contain the letters "sex" (in that order; a search on "exs," for instance, would probably give you a different group of channels indeed—places where sex might even be a four letter word!). Since there are several sex-related channels on IRC, this command can help a new user know what options are out there to choose from; for example, the above command would match #sex, #wetsex and #netsex. (As you'll soon realize, sex is a popular subject on IRC.)

The wildcard "*" at the start *and* end of the phrase means this search string can appear anywhere in the channel name and still match. If you do not find the channel you want using this wildcard search method, try another search with a different but related word. For instance, a search on "*paris*" might fail to bring up any channels, but trying "*franc*" would probably match some French-themed channels (at least the last time I checked).

/flush

Stops long output, such as the output from a general /list command. Analogous to issuing a break command on many machines.

/names

Some consider this command (available on some clients but not all) more interesting than /list. It shows which users are logged on each channel, and whether it is a public or private channel. You should also be able to limit searches by adding arguments, just as you can with other commands; for instance, try the methods outlined earlier for the /list command. For example, you might try **/names -min 5** or **/names <channel-name>** (the <channel-name> argument can contain wildcards if you wish). Here's a small sample of output generated with the /names command:

```
Pub: #hack    zorgo eiji Patrick fup htoaster
Pub: #Nippon  @jircc @miyu_d
Pub: #nicole  MountainD
Pub: #hottub  omar liron beer Deadog moh pfloyd Dode
```

"Pub" means public (or "visible") channel. Other times you might also see "Prv," meaning private. (You will only see this if you are on that private channel. No one can see a private channel except those who are on that particular channel.) Channel names are preceded by the # symbol, while an @ symbol before someone's nickname indicates that he or she is the operator of that channel.

/join <channel-name>

Gets you onto a channel. For, example, the command **/join #romance** will add you to the #romance channel, if it already exists. Everything you type from then on (except commands and private messages, discussed later) will be seen by everyone on #romance. When you are joined to a channel, each of your inputs (the stuff you are saying) is clearly labeled on others' screens by your nickname, so they'll know it's from you. On *your* screen, however, you only see a prompt symbol (like ">"), and not your nick—but hey, only egomaniacs need to see their own name over and over again, right?:-)

If a channel doesn't yet exist when you issue a /join command, it will be created, and you will be its first and only user (until others join it). You'll also be the channel's operator.

Two other things to remember: All channel names must be preceded with the # symbol, and you cannot join a preexisting *private* channel (but who wants to crash a party where you're not invited?).

/kick <channel-name> <nickname>

Forces the specified user off the specified channel. For example, **/kick #coolspot** loudmouth forces the user nicknamed loudmouth off the #coolspot channel. Note that only operators of channels have the authority to issue this command. If you are kicked from a channel, you may still be able to rejoin it, unless you are outright banned.

/mode <channel-name> <option>

Lets you determine the behavior of the channel. Often used right after one creates a new channel, since this is when you are basically the god (or, if you prefer less lofty language, the operator) of this new domain.

The main use for this command is to regulate who can join a channel you've created. For example, **/mode <channel-name>** +s creates a secret channel, while **/mode <channel-name>** +p makes the channel private.

/topic <channel-name> <new-topic>

When you join a channel, you see its current topic. The /topic command lets you change the current topic name of the channel to whatever you want. For example, **/topic #Improv For the Improvisation/Comedy lover in you** would inform those who use the /list command that this channel exists to discuss improvisational comedy.

Some people try to trademark their channel's topic (or at least claim that it is trademarked). To those creative souls I say this: Good luck trying to enforce it! (The Internet is still too much of an anarchistic cyberwildwest for that, at least for now.)

/who

If you are joined to a channel, this command lists all users on that channel. If you're not on any channel, the listing includes everyone on IRC at the time this command was issued. Warning: During busy periods (and when is IRC not?) using this command without an argument when you are not on a channel could result in a list with a heck of a lot of names. This is another example of why there is a strong argument for using arguments with most IRC commands. Below are some useful variants of the command.

/who <channel-name>

Lists who is on the specified channel, along with the host address (where a person logs in from) and channel status of each "channeler." For example, **/who #neatstuff** would display the address of every IRCer on the channel #neatstuff.

/who *

When you first get on a channel, a list of nicknames is shown, representing all those on the channel. The **/who *** command gives you more information for those people joined to the current channel.

/who <nickname>

Displays information about the person with the specified nickname.

/who *<search-string>*

You can use wildcards to search for others on IRC. For instance, since most people at UCLA have the letters "ucla" somewhere in their official electronic address, you could try /who *ucla* if you wanted to find all people on IRC at UCLA. (All users are, in a sense, "marked" by the address they logged in from.) If you were not sure what University of California campus the person you want is from, you could widen the search, changing the search string "ucla" to "uc" and doing another wildcard /who command. Conversely, adding *more* characters to the string would limit the search. You get the idea.

/whois <nickname>

Displays the real name and, in many cases, the login name and address of a specific IRC user; often used to see who is online. For example, /whois babyface would provide information for the person using the nickname babyface, whereas /whois * would list the information for everybody on every channel. Once again, such simple commands can generate much more output than you probably desire, so be careful.

If the person you want to chat with has changed nicknames or is not currently on IRC, an error message appears (e.g., "babyface: No Such Nickname"). If this error does occur, try the following related command.

/whowas <nickname>

Outputs info about the person who most recently used the indicated nickname. Similar to /whois, but deals with the past (people who recently signed off IRC) instead of the present. In a way it acts like the *69 call-tracing feature that some telephone users have access to today (for uncovering the number of someone who just called but hung up).

/msg <nickname> <message>

Sends a private message to the IRC user with the indicated nickname. For instance, the command /**msg cooldood Want to go to a new channel?** would make the text "Want to go to a new channel?" appear on cooldood's screen, but no one else's. It would be preceded by my nickname sandwiched by asterisks (assuming I was the one who sent this message). If my nick were "ircqtguy," the message would look like this on cooldood's computer screen: "*ircqtguy* Want to go to a new channel?"

On most systems, you can also try putting more than one nickname before the message, in a kind of "nickname list." Try this if you want the private message to go to more than one user.

/msg , <message>

Sends a message to the last person who sent *you* a message.

/msg . <message>

Sends a message to the last person you sent a message to.

/query <nickname-list>

Sends all new messages (those after this /query command) to the specified people (with names given in your "nickname list"). Generally used to set up and enter into a private conversation with the folks you have listed (in most cases, it's just one other IRC user). Every message you type after issuing the /query command will go only to the person(s) you listed. This can be a big time and stress saver, since otherwise you'd have to issue a /msg command for each private message you wanted to send to the user(s) you want to chat with.

If the nickname list consists of only one IRCer, and that person then also issues the /query command, using only your nickname as the <nickname-list> argument, then you have established a private conversation. While in query mode, you and the other person(s) can continue to *listen* to the discussion on whatever public channels you're on, although you and the other user(s) will not be able to respond to any of the messages there (until you exit query mode).

To exit query mode, type /**query** all by itself.

/me <action>

Sends an action description to the channel you are on. Appears flush left in the channel window, without any bracketed labels—but it does begin with your nickname. That is, the "/me" part will be replaced with your current nick when the line of text (i.e., the <action> argument) actually appears on the channel.

This command can be used as a kind of virtual analog to body language. For instance, if you are laughing at someone's last comment, you can enter /**me laughs and rolls on the floor**. Or, if someone compliments you, you might send the action /**me bows with gratitude**. For you drama buffs and scriptwriters, think of this command as allowing you to write a kind of simple "scene description" to complement the usual dialogue.

/set novice off

Allows you to join more than one channel. Reading and interacting with multiple channels simultaneously can get really confusing, which is why keeping the novice setting *on* may actually be a better move, especially for "newbie-ginners."

/invite <nickname> <channel-name>

Asks another IRCer to join you in a conversation. For example, /**invite happypat #coolspot** would send a message to the user nicknamed happypat, asking him or her (you never know for sure on IRC!) to join you on the #coolspot channel. The channel name is optional. Note that this is the only way one can join invite-only channels.

/ignore <address-or-nickname> all

Ignore all messages from the indicated e-mail address, or from the person with the indicated nickname. Parts of the argument can be a wild-card character; for instance, the command **/ignore *@well.com** ignores all messages from those with accounts at well.com.

To turn off this ignore feature, issue the same command, but use the argument "none" rather than "all" after the address or nickname.

/summon <address>

Asks somebody connected to a host system that has IRC to join you on IRC. You must use the person's entire e-mail address. For instance, **/summon MCicemilk@x.y.com** would send a message to the user named MCicemilk (who is currently on the machine labeled x.y.com on the Internet) asking him or her to connect to IRC. Remember that it's not the best idea to summon people unless you know they're probably amenable to the idea—otherwise you may wind up annoying them. Also note that this command does not work on all sites.

/leave <channel-name>

There may be 50 ways to leave your lover, but you don't need to remember that many ways to leave an IRC channel. The above command should suffice. For example, to leave the channel #love, issue the command **/leave #love** (just don't mention this to Barbara DeAngelis or Leo Buscaglia). This puts you back in the "IRC limbo" you started at when you first got onto IRC; from there, you can /join some other channel if you wish.

/part <channel-name>

Same effect as /leave.

/away <message>

Use this command when you have to go away for a while, but don't want to disconnect from IRC. It lets others know you're still connected but temporarily away from your terminal/computer.

After you issue this command, the list generated by a /who command will display a *G* (for *gone*) next to your nickname instead of an *H* (for *here*). In addition, any IRCer who attempts to send you a private message—or enter a /whois command about you—will get a reply stating the message you indicated. The message argument can fill in more details about why you are away—such as "getting lunch" or, if you've had a nervous breakdown, "out to lunch." To stop the effect of this command (like when you return from being away), just enter **/away** without any message argument.

/quit <message>

Takes you out of IRC. (Now you can catch your breath. Congratulations—you made it out alive!) The message argument is optional (i.e., you still quit if there's no message). A typical message might inform all the channels you are on that your royal presence will soon vanish from their midst (your message goes to all the channels you are currently on before you actually exit IRC via this command).

/bye <message>

Same effect as /quit <message>.

/exit

Same effect as /quit.

/signoff

Same effect as /quit.

Entering, Tracking & Saving Text

So now you know basic concepts and commands—but what about this input text I keep mentioning? How and where does one enter the commands and dialogue, and keep track of it, as well as inputs from other IRCers on a channel?

There are a few main areas (generally two to three, depending on your IRC client) where you interact with your client in order to enter text, watch it appear on a channel, track others' comments, and scroll back to earlier happenings on the channel.

The first screen area is what I refer to as the *general output window*. It displays the general stuff that is output by the server you are connected to—text either generated on its own (e.g., a server's welcome message) or as a result of commands you give to it (e.g., /list). This is generally the first window to appear after your client is launched.

Then there is the *input area*, where you type in your next line of dialogue or your next command. (Don't forget that most menu-based IRC clients also let you enter some commands from their menus.) Some of you, like those using a Mac-based IRC client, will use the small window created by the client specifically to accept inputs. For other IRCers, like those using certain Windows-based clients, your input area is just the top or bottom line (usually the bottom) of the general output window discussed above.

With many clients, the input area consists of a single line. If you type more than one line (e.g., of dialogue) without a break or return, it should still wind up intact on the channel, but you might not be able to see earlier lines as you're inputting. (For example, in my client's input window, only the current line is visible to me as I compose inputs.) The upshot: keep it short and sweet!

If you make a mistake you can edit to correct it, but once you hit Return or Enter, it's too late—it's out in cyberspace now! That is, the characters you typed are sent to the IRC server for processing (it either responds if you entered a command, or sends the text to the channel you are on if your input is not a command). If it's not a command, all those on your channel will be able to read your input, even if it still has mistakes—so be careful when composing your lines. After you hit Return, the input area clears and is ready for your next line.

Another window—which I refer to as the *channel window*—shows the ongoing conversation taking place on the channel you are joined to. When you /join #coolchann, a window entitled #coolchann is created and displayed on your screen (the exact appearance of this window or area may vary for some clients). From the moment you join the channel to the moment you exit, everything that anyone on #coolchann says will be shown in that window, each line labeled with the appropriate user nick. The output from your own typing also appears in the channel window, in addition to the text being typed by the other members of the channel. (Also note that many clients allow you to enter commands or text in the channel window itself, augmenting the "input area" method of entering commands and text discussed earlier.)

Since the channel window can fill up fast, make sure your client is configured so that old text is saved into a buffer. This way, the text "scrolls up" (or back, if you prefer) into the buffer as new lines appear, and you can scroll up in the window whenever you wish to see earlier stuff said while you've been on the channel. This buffering and scrolling is a great aid to help you watch and participate in ongoing conversations.

When you leave a channel, its corresponding window will most likely disappear—as does the scroll buffer (which saves the dialogue that occurred while you were on that channel), in clients like the one I use. Hence, if you can, you should save your text into *log files* that get stored on your machine's hard disk. Most IRC clients should let you save log files, and some have documentation files or online help to assist you. When channel windows go away, the log files would still be around, so you can analyze your IRC sessions at your convenience. (Excerpts from log files appear in the next chapter.)

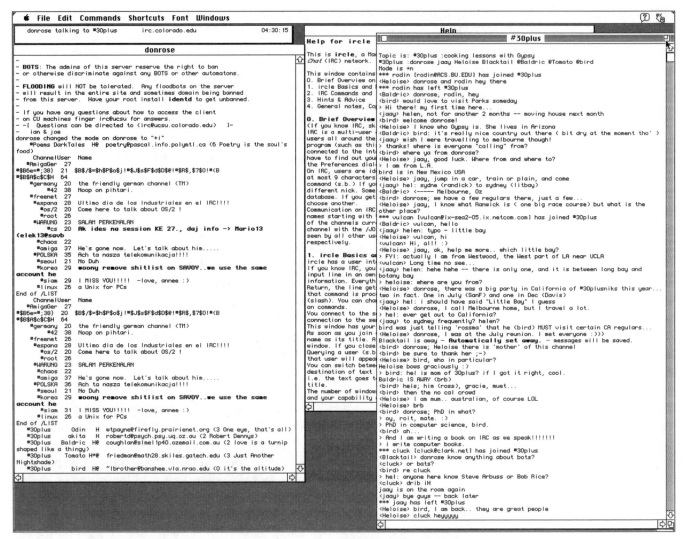

Figure 3-2: *The ircle client for the Mac, displaying a small input window (top left), a general output window (left), a help window (background) and a channel window (right).*

Figure 3-2 shows a snapshot of a computer screen that includes all of the window types discussed above. Notice that a help window appears in the background as well; this pops up when you enter the /help command on my client (which happens to be ircle, as you can tell from the help window's text). Other clients may respond to /help in a different manner, but in all cases some useful information should be presented to you in one of your client's windows.

Quick Advice for Initial IRC Explorations

Now that I've told you about useful concepts, essential commands and the basic mechanics of how to enter and track dialogue, you might wonder if that's all you need to know. To quote John McLaughlin, "Wrong!" To help prepare you even more, and give you a bit larger perspective on things, here's a sampling of basic advice—a few essential rules of thumb that new IRCers will find useful.

- Use log files to help you find things you may have missed in the heat of typing and reading. I recommend saving every part of your early IRC sessions—both to learn from them, and to catch some of the gems you may have missed (e.g., you may have been focusing on one or two channelers while ignoring interesting exchanges that others were having).

- Don't use someone else's nickname. Pretty much common sense—but many great rules of advice are. Not only would "nick duplication" be confusing, but whoever had the name first would be upset. The last thing you want when new to an area on the Net is to get people upset at you right away! Check the name list that appears right after you join a channel, and simply avoid using those names. And don't use a name you saw on a channel you were recently on. Of course, it's impossible to be sure a name is not in use *somewhere* on the thousands of IRC channels, but picking a nick that is unique to you—your life and interests, your personality, your sense of humor—plus avoiding obvious names that anyone could dream up, will help lower the odds that someone else has used the nickname you want.

- Write as fast as is feasible, keeping sentences short and to the point. If you type slowly and/or try to compose overly long messages, comments from others might flood the channel in the meantime (and capture the attention of the others on that channel). The quicker you enter text, the better the chance that it will appear in the channel window right after the line you are responding to. If you wait too long to reply or the line takes too long to enter, others may not make the connection, and your words might appear out of place or out of context.

- Precede direct comments to a particular user by that user's nickname (for example, **cooldood: the answer is seven**). If you don't, your input might be misinterpreted by other users, and/or missed by the intended recipient—especially if channel traffic is heavy. You could also be suave and smooth and include the name in your sentence in a more natural-sounding way, but the general "<nickname>: <your-input>" structure is more common because it saves time, and the name is easier to spot.

- Spelling errors are frequent and often on purpose, so don't get overly English-teacherish about such mistakes. Many people just want to get thoughts across as quickly and directly as possible on IRC; doing things like entering "sux" instead of "sucks" helps accomplish this. This leads to my next byte of advice:

- Learn and get used to as much IRC "cyberese" (such as the abbreviations and shortcut vernacular that others use) as you can. Any new language idiosyncrasies will sink in fast; just be open to it. Remember the old saying: When in cyberRome, do as the cyberRomans do. (See the glossary at the back of this book for more about IRC-related cyberese.)

- Never type in something if you don't understand the input or don't know what it does. Be especially wary if someone else asked you to type it. As we all know, blind obedience can be dangerous at times. Think of this advice as equivalent to rules for giving out your credit card number. For all you know, some unkind Netter may be trying to get you to give him or her control of your client!

- When in doubt about something related to IRC, don't be shy about asking for help. Try joining a help channel like #irchelp. IRC operators often hang out there, and some might be willing to answer your queries. (You may need to do a **/list *help*** or **/list *irc*** if the spelling is slightly different for some reason.) Also, see Chapter 6 for detailed descriptions of various help channels (and many others).

- Keep reading this book! In Chapter 5, I provide more advice about saying and doing things properly while cyberchatting.

Don't worry if it all seems a bit overwhelming at first. Like all things in life (except death and taxes), you'll get used to it. For example, you may often see several people on the same channel carrying on multiple conversations. This may be disorienting, especially when first encountered. Imagine if you were at a crowded party (in real space and time, not IRC) and suddenly lost the ability to focus your hearing on someone; now you start to get the idea! Eventually, you will go with the flow, and will relearn that focusing ability in this new medium. Since IRCing is a skill, it can be made perfect with practice.

Moving On

By now, you know a lot—but you may be asking questions like, for instance, "What does an actual IRC session look like?" Coincidentally, the next chapter deals with this very question. I've always felt that learning by example helps one's understanding, and in Chapter 4 I'll present and discuss excerpts from a couple of actual IRC logs, so you can learn firsthand how things operate.

ANATOMY OF A CHAT SESSION

In this chapter, you get to learn by example. Why? Because it's fun and you'll absorb a lot. How? By following along with my analysis of a couple of instructive IRC session excerpts. I'll provide commentary to help you understand what is going on as we "walk through" segments of log files recorded during my own actual IRC sessions. You'll be able to see in a practical context many of the things we've covered in previous chapters, and hopefully you'll pick up a few new things, too.

In the Beginning: Starting an IRC Session

When my IRC client connects to IRC, it automatically opens the general output window and the input window. In the general output window, welcome messages from the server appear. Following is the welcome I received when I connected to a server in Boston. The message, including channel statistics and official server policies, is typical of the welcome most IRC servers give you when you first connect to a site.

```
*** Welcome to the Internet Relay Network don-rose
*** This server was created Sun Nov 20 1994 at 11:36:25 EST
Mode flags for users are: oiws; for channels are: biklmnopstv
There are 3558 users and 1942 invisible on 86 servers
There are 82 operator(s) online
There are 1632 channels formed
I have 294 clients and 2 servers
- cs-pub.bu.edu Message of the Day -
- 21/7/1994 18:28
- Rules on this server:
-
- (1) This rule is not negotiable.
-    .   ..__.  .__ .__..___.  __.  I
-   |\ ||  |  [__)|  |  |  (_  I
-   | \||__| [__)|__|  |  .__) *
-
- (2) You may not use an illegal user@host on this server.
- If I find you using an illegal user@host and you do not
- give a reason that I find acceptable, I will /kill you.
-
- (3) Disclaimer: This IRC server is provided as a service.
- Myself (Helen Rose, hrose@cs.bu.edu) and Boston University's
- Computer Science Department take no responsibility and
- explicitly disclaim any legal liability for the content of
- any messages that pass through this server, and the results
- of running any commands which you do as a result of being on
- irc.
-
- Any questions to hrose@cs.bu.edu
```

At this point, I was officially on IRC, but I still had not joined to any channels. It's a kind of IRC limbo. If I'd typed something within my input area at this point, then hit Enter, the words would have vanished into thin cyberair. My input can only be seen by others when I'm officially joined to a channel, using the /join command.

In fact, once upon a time, the message "You are not connected to a server" actually came up first on my screen (that is, this was the first line in my general window before the usual welcome message). Why? Because I tried to enter a command (in my input area) before I was actually connected to a server. The moral of the story: remember to wait until after you get your welcome message to enter commands.

Let's look at another typical IRC server welcome message. Figure 4-1 shows the beginning of one of my sessions using a server in Colorado.

Notice that bots are discouraged on both the Boston and Colorado servers. However, the Colorado server is not as adamant as the other site is. That is, the irc.colorado.edu site does not forbid bots, but they can take action at any time to deal with them if necessary. Flooding is also mentioned here; some of the "bad bots" that have appeared on IRC in the past got their bad rep (or is it rap?) by generating tons of text (i.e., flooding). Thus, the Colorado ops warn that this behavior in particular is being watched for.

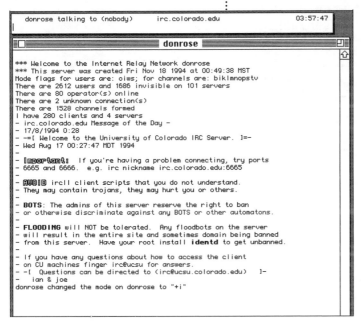

Figure 4-1: *My general output window right after connecting to my preferred server. Notice the window's name (the same as my nickname). The small area above is the input window.*

/List & Learn

Let's continue analyzing my Colorado session. Just after the welcome message, I entered the command **/list -min 10** into my input window, in order to see which channels had at least 10 people on them. Below is the resulting list (some parts were revised or reformatted for clarity and brevity). The list appeared (as do most command responses) in my general output window. Note that the command lines themselves are not always echoed on this screen—you might only see the result of whatever command you issued. Note also that in channel lists like the example below, the text listed to the right of the number of users is the channel's topic, even though the heading may say "Name."

```
Channel       Users  Name
#kyutech       13
#$BE13$(B      16
#$B6e=#;38}    15
*              10
#$BLV4IM}(     14
#$B#C#V(B      12
#$B$_$"(B      18
#$B$A$c$C$H    49
#kasvua        12    hällä väliä
#Oulu          14
#lut           10
#kala          15
#tahitibar     16
#Norge         12
#kana          16
#scs           10
```

```
#DigiStad      10    irc-sint-party gifjes! aaargh
#dutch         11
#latvia        10    Kokaiins sexa laikaa rulz ;-D (c) GUNA
#magyar        10
#francaise     11
#blujoker      11    "Hey where the hek is everybody?"
#alpha         12
*              49
#europe        13    Daze wants someone to hit
#kerala        12
#colombia      12
#AtlAntic.cA 14
#florida       14
#francais      24    Lague
#texas         19    where is everyone?
#Croatia       10
#sweden        15
*              19
#lonely        10
#hi            10    hi all
#germany       14    Scroll Hoelle
#russian       27    Pozdno, Sofka, raskrili... ;-)
#41plus        15    New Lakota saying: "It is a Good Day to Split"...
#Brasil        26
#france        37
#irchelp       11
#tw            21    /server bart.ugcs.caltech.edu for a good time
#siam          17
#punk          13    F**k it all
```

#moscow	12	Pochem opium dlja naroda?
#ireland	15	
#laos	18	Today it's not a good day
#eu-opers	18	
#hello	20	NEW & improved uses of the grunt Inquire within
#manila	11	
#ARGENTINA	13	
#hottub	16	ah, the joys of lag....
#chat	27	barron: gi0 wants the -sh**ty!
#freenet	34	
#bored	11	Ur moms
#singles	32	
#canada	21	W0lf + Waterbed + ChristmasLights = *HUBBA HUBBA*
#teensex	14	MONTY PYTHON RUUULES!! :)
#initgame	16	Lag is boring...let's play on anyway
#seoul	23	ROCKIN DA HOUSE!
#cool	11	
#penang	10	#penang alive again!!! :)
#linux	20	Goto Linuxnet... finger linuxnet@kia.xensei.com
#os/2	25	Web explorer 0.93 is on ftp.ibm.net /pub/WebExplorer/
#bearcave	15	Home of the Furry, Fuzzy Guys and the Men Who Love 'Em
#30plus	22	split-city
#talk	30	Let me out of this cheap B-movie!
#chinese	28	
#cambodia	18	"Life is grand, dont take it for granted"
#spanking	18	Adult spanking Forum come on in !!!!
#malaysia	17	astaghfirullah
#boggle	10	Boggle
#penpals	22	THE LAGGED BUT STILL FRIENDLY CHANNEL!!

#palestine	10	The Language is Arabic
#Bawel	49	Final exam is coming to town!
#truthdare	18	An Adult Game of Truth or Dare - /msg TDHelp helpme
#disney	18	What's your favorite color? Red. NO BLUE!
#singapore	17	Eldar dam sian lor !!!!!!!
#cricket	16	I 546/9d WI 15/1; Z 166/9 A 167/8; SL238/5 AR101*
#appleiigs	10	BIG ASS HAM!!!
#netsex	64	Marais you are a great woman :)
#israel	15	knee problems discussion
#bisex	19	Also available on Undernet! /manhattan.ks.us.underne
#-sex-	14	DEEZ LuVs YA
#polonia	11	no nie
#gam	11	soon available: nude gif from <bic> :)
#hawaii	15	Welcome to Hawaii
#polska	24	zapraszamy wszystkich jutro na imprezke do lublina
#bdsm	27	The #BDSM Opera Co. presents Strauss's "Salome beheads
#espanol	41	kewea
#mindvox	11	The Cliquesr Undergrount Network Team
#taiwan	28	/server bart.ugcs.caltech.edu join another NET !
#nippon	22	The probibility someone sees you is proportional
#usa	22	"I want to world to know that Wildthing loves
#gaysex	33	Gaysex: Where ON ONE gets a 2nd chance
#netbsd	14	
#perl	17	
#mtg	11	Magic : The Gathering
#beijing	18	Welcome to Beijing! :)
#nin	11	TRENT IS *NOT* HERE.
#talk2me	11	Where'd everybody go?
*	14	

```
#warung        22    Finnaly dapat gak op
#Korea         50    HAS ANYONE SEEN PUPPET!!!???
#35plus        11    The friendly channel for people 35-ish or older
#marathon      10    FileServ's cmdchar is % (temporary)
#chaos         13    Bot gone!!  Lagged more than ice_man on a cold day!
*              14
#macintosh     21    MacTCP v2.0.6 is released...
#nicecafe      11    This channel is not silent, we all have ESP
#www           16    World Wide Web (HTML, Mozilla, Mosaic, Lynx, etc).
#islam         19    Islam is the way
#friendly      23    Arena's first day!
#amiga         43    Well, this is a fine mess here today!
#china         16    Duckie:dont make ur bot mass deop the channel
#jordan        11    Salam
#viet          66    MISS U GIRL
#india         45    Photography
#unix          26    We are no substitute for your man pages!
#iran          11    khosh.amadid.....
#root          39    Computer Systems, Languages, Programming, and Arch
#kuwait        15    harhor like you all
End of /LIST
```

Quite a long list, but not nearly as long as the thousands of lines that can result from a plain ol' no-argument /list command! There are always lots of channels with several people on them. Part of the reason for this constant activity is that IRC operates 24 hours a day, all over the world, and there is always someplace on earth where people are not sleeping.

Each time you log in to IRC, you can do a /list command with various-sized search arguments (I happened to use 10 in my example) to gauge the relative popularity of various channels. If a certain channel always seems to have a lot of users on it, you can probably deduce that it is fairly popular. What makes a channel popular with IRCers? Try them out and judge for yourself (or check out Chapter 6 for an in-depth look at various channels).

A channel with a particular theme may change names over time, or several channels with similar themes may exist simultaneously. For example, take the theme of IRC help. The #irchelp channel (shown in bold in the list above) is usually present, but at other times the more popular help channel might be #help, and some help channels may even go by other monikers. The upshot: look around diligently to discover channels with similar themes, using topic names to help you guide your search. If there are more than one, try each for a while until you get what you need to get out of it.

Also, remember your search criteria when you look through your list for channels. For instance, the #help channel is not listed in my example above—but it still may be present, with fewer than 10 folks on it. To make sure of the existence or nonexistence of any channel, do a search with less limiting criteria (but be prepared for even greater torrents of text scrolling across your screen!).

Don't worry about the channels (mostly at the beginning of a /list output) that have strange characters in their names. There always seem to be a few of these. The "*" channels, for instance, are private (off-limits to the general public). And some IRCers use odd-looking channel names when they wish to keep semi-permanent channels alive yet discourage anyone outside their group from accidentally wandering onto their turf. An unusual character string can also help to ensure that the name of a channel will remain unique (remember that if a channel goes away and someone later creates one with the same name, that new person now controls that channel and its name). Of course, if you absolutely must know the answer to this riddle of odd channel names, you can always try to join such channels and ask for yourself!

There are lots of topics out there that are "out there." And I mean from funny to funky. Still, most topic names help describe not only the content of channels, but also the tone (e.g., serious or lighthearted, open to all or mainly closed to outsiders) and even the language of choice. Sometimes the topic can serve as a kind of alluring headline, giving some snippet of new news that might attract IRCers onto the channel to discuss the news or other items. For instance, when the example /list was generated, the #macintosh channel (also shown in bold above) had the topic "MacTCP v2.0.6 is released." This may be Greek to Windows geeks (no offense, Gates-based gurus), but to Mac-based Netters this indicates a new version of communications software vital to optimal IRC usage—so it should help draw Mac IRCers on to discuss this news or learn more about what it means for them.

Speaking of #macintosh on IRC, this channel happens to be the main focus of the next section. After a quick stop on the #30plus channel, I'll show portions of one of my sessions on #macintosh, and provide running commentary to help you follow along.

An Annotated IRC Log

Now I want to give you a taste of what a typical chat session looks like. To do that, I'll present excerpts from two actual IRC log files. I've edited the files for clarity and brevity, and have interspersed comments about the session throughout.

To prepare yourself for this journey, start by imagining that your login to IRC went well (using the information provided in earlier chapters), and that you're finally on IRC. Now, for convenience, pretend you're me, with the nickname "donrose." (I chose this nick to make the session clearer for you, but remember that, in most cases, IRCers don't use their real names as online nicks.)

```
▦▦▦▦▦▦▦▦▦▦▦▦▦▦#30plus▦▦▦▦▦▦▦▦▦▦▦▦
Topic is: #30plus :cooking lessons with Gypsy
#30plus :donrose jaay Heloise Blacktail @Baldric @Tomato @bird
Mode is +n
*** rodin [rodin@ACS.BU.EDU] has joined #30plus
<Heloise> donrose and rodin hey there
*** rodin has left #30plus
<Baldric> donrose, rodin, hey
<bird> would love to visit Parks someday
> Hi there! my first time here...
<jaay> helen, not for another 2 months -- moving house next month
<bird> welcome donrose!
<Heloise> I know who Gypsy is. She lives in Arizona
<Baldric> bird: it's really nice country out there ( bit dry at the moment tho' )
<jaay> wish I were travelling to melbourne though!
> thanks! where is everyone "calling" from?
<bird> where ya from donrose?
<Heloise> jaay, good luck. Where from and where to?
> I am from L.A.
bird is in New Mexico USA
<Heloise> jaay, jump in a car, train or plain, and come
<jaay> hel: sydne (randick) to sydney (litbay)
<Baldric> <----- Melbourne, Oz
<bird> donrose; we have a few regulars there, just a few...
<Heloise> jaay, I know what Ranwick is ( one big race course) but what is the
other place?
*** vulcan [vulcan@ix-sea2-05.ix.netcom.com] has joined #30plus
<Baldric> vulcan, hello
<jaay> helen: typo - little bay
<Heloise> vulcan, hi
<vulcan> Hi, all! :)
<Heloise> jaay, ok, help me more.. which little bay?
> FYI: actually I am from Westwood, the West part of LA near UCLA
<vulcan> Long time no see...
<jaay> helen: hehe hehe -- there is only one, and it is between long bay and
botany bay
> heloise: where are you from?
<Heloise> donrose, there was a big party in California of #30plusniks this year...
two in fact. One in July (SanF) and one in Dec (Davis)
<jaay> hel: i should have said "Little Bay" I guess
<Heloise> donrose, I call Melbourne home, but I travel a lot.
> hel: ever get out to California?
<jaay> to sydney frequently? helen?
bird was just telling 'rossma' that he (bird) MUST visit certain CA regulars...
<Heloise> donrose, I was at the July reunion. I met everyone :)))
Blacktail is away - Automatically set away. - messages will be saved.
<bird> donrose; Heloise there is 'mother' of this channel
<bird> be sure to thank her ;-)
<Heloise> bird, who in particular?
Heloise bows graciously :)
> bird: hel is mom of 30plus? if I got it right, cool.
Baldric IS AWAY (brb)
<bird> hels; him (ross), gracie, muet...
<bird> then the no cal crowd
<Heloise> I am mum.. australian, of course LOL
<Heloise> brb
<bird> donrose; PhD in what?
> oy, roit, mate. :)
> PhD in computer science, bird.
<bird> ah...
> And I am writing a book on IRC as we speak!!!!!!!
> i write computer books.
*** cluck [cluck@clark.net] has joined #30plus
<Blacktail> donrose know anything about bots?
<cluck> or bats?
<bird> re cluck
> hel: anyone here know Steve Arbuss or Bob Rice?
<cluck> drib iH
jaay is on the roam again
<jaay> bye guys -- back later
*** jaay has left #30plus
<Heloise> bird, I am back.. they are great people
<Heloise> cluck heyyyyy
```

Figure 4-2: *A snapshot of my initial interactions on the #30plus channel.*

Next, you might do what I used to do all the time: refresh yourself on some basic help information by issuing the /help command. You might then join a channel such as #30plus—one of my favorites, because of its friendliness and regular visitors.

Figure 4-2 shows what my channel window looked like after some initial dialogue on #30plus. You can glance at the second line to see which IRCers were on #30plus at the time; a nick list is always given whenever you join a channel. Also note how people's entrances and exits are marked by announcement lines, each beginning with a string of asterisks. Nicknames are given in both directions, but a user's e-mail address is only broadcast upon entering. Also note how my text is not preceded by my nick (just the > symbol), since we are looking at a snapshot of my own channel window. Lines of text that begin with a user's nickname *without* brackets are actions or descriptive facts provided by that user. Following is Heloise's response to one of bird's remarks (suggesting that I thank her for being the "mother" of #30plus):

```
Heloise bows graciously :)
```

The smiley at the end probably means Hel is trying to diffuse the seriousness that some might infer from her bow. Of course, text goes by so fast on crowded IRC channels that meaning is not always correctly processed the first time, and it is possible Hel meant something I didn't pick up on (by the bow and/or the smiley). The point is that you never know for sure what another is thinking or trying to convey while on

IRC, but the longer you use IRC the better you get at this task (and the discussions often are not so crucial that it matters all that much).

After leaving the #30plus channel, I sometimes like to try a channel with a little different flavor to it. Going from social to technical is a nice change, so I might try the #macintosh channel (since the Mac is the machine I use, for IRC and other things). The rest of this first walk-through will involve this computer-oriented channel.

After I entered the command /**join #macintosh,** a new channel window with the name #macintosh appeared on my desktop. The following text appeared in that window:

```
Topic is: #macintosh :ftp://ftp.amug.org/pub/pentium-jokes.txt
#macintosh :donrose _5150_ ScottT MASH timbo Tamer ynnus wrath
meerkat mellow Tsunami @SbizZ BradK @Doppler dwight @Wowbagger
@TheBard @MacServ
```

Note the reference to a "Pentium jokes" file in the topic name. Topic names, as I mentioned earlier, are often not really names at all, but rather phrases, often funny or jokey in style. Sometimes they are informative (in this case the topic at least does contain the word Macintosh), but mostly they simply give you an idea of the tone of the channel and personality of its regular denizens.

Listed next was the channel name, followed by the nicknames of the people on the channel. The folks whose nicks begin with the @ sign are the channel operators. Note that I had to edit out some names because...well, let's just say that there's often greater freedom of word usage online than in books or TV (a freedom I applaud wholeheartedly).

At this point, I sat back and waited for others' conversations to start spilling into my channel window (which usually occurs in mid-discussion, as if you just walked in on a lively party). It didn't take long:

```
<mellow> man I can't even stick in a 3rd party CD-ROM drive cuz no
one makes face plates...LAME!
<Tamer> mellow you know in the powerbooks there a fuse for the
power manager... now apple can only replace it by replacing
the mother board
```

Note how the names appear in brackets before each line of text, indicating which user is saying which lines of dialogue. As I expected, I joined the channel right smack in the middle of an ongoing conversation, in this case the one that mellow and Tamer are having. Also notice the minimal use of capitalization; many IRCers, especially those who've used chat for quite a while, refrain from capitalizing things as much as possible, to save typing time (and strength!—kinda like saving your breath during a heated spoken exchange).

```
<timbo> there are heaps of faceplates
> Anyone know if a 3x speed CDroom is really that much better than 2x ?
```

This last line was my first input to the channel. (Note that since it's my log file, recorded from a session using my client, no name precedes any of my sentences—just the > symbol—though the others on the channel do see my nick on their screens). I felt this was a reasonable first question to ask, since technical discussions are the norm on #macintosh. However, this line might seem odd and off-putting if it appeared on a social channel like, say, #netsex. The point or lesson here: IRCers must take into account the types of people who tend to populate a channel when composing messages; especially be careful with the first few lines you send to the channel, when others' first impressions of you are being formed.

In the next few lines, three users left the channel:

```
*** Signoff: meerkat [<email address deleted>]
*** Signoff: MASH [<email address deleted>]
*** Signoff: ynnus [<email address deleted>]
```

People may sign on or off at will; in this case, a few folks left. (I know these address deletions may seem a bit like *Dragnet*, but I had to protect the privacy, if not the innocent.)

In the next line, mellow answered my question about CD-ROM (even though I misspelled the word in my first input above). It's generally a good idea to precede a response with the nick of the person you are responding to (as mellow did here), otherwise it can be hard to tell that someone's talking to you (like finding the proverbial needle in a haystack). This becomes more important as more people are on the channel, and as more inputs pile up on the screen after the initial line you're responding to.

```
<mellow> donrose: no.
> Cool... thanks. Seems a lot extra dough for the
> 3x; 2x seems std today.
<_5150_> cd what?
> CDrom
<mellow> I want a mini-tower case for my mac.
<_5150_> oh..
<mellow> like a PC case...
<Tamer> what's a good 2x CD-drive?
> good cdrom: NEC drives.
<mellow> tamer: any...they're all the same now...
*** Prankster [<email address deleted>] has joined #macintosh
```

A Log's Life The sessions discussed in this chapter were captured from the channel window used during my IRC session. The captured files are generally referred to as "log files." I recommend saving as much as you can into such files, so you can go back over them after you depart IRC and see how your sessions went, learn some lessons where you can, etc. It's often difficult in the midst of a session to really see the overall patterns and the many discussions that are going on, since you are probably busy typing away and thinking up responses, questions, comments, how to spell certain words, and so on. This is even more true if the number of people on the channel is high, or if you are a newbie to IRC.

Of course, some IRCers just like log files for the automatic memories they provide—kind of like a text-only camcorder. This probably increases in importance if you're using IRC for dating and romance. On a more serious note, those using IRC for business or research conferencing can use log files as minutes of meetings or notes to go over after conference time.

Notice in the last line that IRC announces not only when folks leave, but also when people first appear on a channel. This means it is harder to lurk in the background on a channel without being noticed. (This is not the case in other parts of the Net—like USENET, where you can lurk undetected by reading newsgroups without ever posting messages to them.)

```
<mellow> NEC = too expensive for a CD-ROM
<timbo> or sony
<mellow> NEC = #1 monitor though.
<timbo> less problems with drivers on the sony, unless you use
NEC drivers
*** Prankster has left #macintosh
*** Quatro [<email address deleted>] has joined #macintosh
> tamer and mellow: best CDrom drive for price: mail order Mac
> catalogs (I saw one with a $189 price)
<Tamer> how about the cheap ones.. the ones that run for $199?
<mellow> donrose: just make sure it's around 280ms access
time...not like 500ms...
> MacWArehouse had one for $199, with MBG and they are well known,
> not flybynite
<mellow> CD-ROM needs a LOT of help...man, the f***in' thing is
READ only, it could be faster!
<mellow> it's a industry scam...
```

Note that the appearance of a bit of profanity and candid opinions (e.g., in the last two sentences) are not unusual events on IRC; in fact, some say it is the norm. I personally don't have a problem with this, and often find it refreshing, but be forewarned if this sort of thing is not for you. Again, you must realize that the Internet is like the Wild West all over again—but taking place on an electronic frontier this time around.

```
> There are CACHE programs you can buy to increase speed
> on cdroms
<mellow> donrose: if you retrieve data off the CD-ROM that's NOT
repetitive, you won't notice a speed difference.
> correct
<mellow> yeah..for programs that access the same files on the CD-ROM.
<mellow> cuz it basically copies to your hard drive while yer not
looking!
> what if you copy the CD's files onto a fast hard drive? will the
> file (program) run much faster?????
<mellow> donrose: if you have a spare 650 meg HD laying around,
and you copied your entire CD ROM·to the HD, the program
would kick ass.
> mellow: so if I keep a 650MB HD around, and only use each time I
> wanna use a CD (copy, use, delete) then I'd be in good shape...
*** Vicious [<email address deleted>] has joined #macintosh
*** _5150_ has left #macintosh
<Vicious> mellow : what do you think of Newton's ?
<mellow> Vicious: cool toys...
<mellow> donrose: yeah.but it takes a long time to copy.
<Vicious> mellow:their pretty cheap now too - sub $200
<mellow> Vicious: my friend has one....he like it...just the
handwriting rec. sux rocks...
```

Note that mellow's last reply to me (shown in bold above) came after
answering Vicious; if mellow had not preceded the line with my nick, I
might not have known the line was meant for me—especially since he
had just replied to Vicious. Sure, I might have figured things out okay
from the context or content, but adding my name made things easier
and faster to process.

Also notice the presence of words like "sux" (short for "sucks") and "cuz" (short for "because"), and other abbreviations or cyberslang that appear on channels—more examples of how people often reengineer their language in various ways on the Internet. This is often done because typing fast is important, particularly when that is your only means of communicating for what is often many hours nonstop.

Naturally, the above text is just a small sampling of IRC life, only one excerpt of one channel's activity (and edited down a bit as well!), but it should leave you with an initial flavor and help you as you read the coming sections and chapters.

Multichannel Chatting

Below is an example of what being on more than one channel (two in this case) can look like, using an excerpt from another log file. This is a log file from a new (IRC-spawned) friend of mine, Gregor (quite a good poet, actually), whom I met while on the #poems channel. After we spent a good deal of time on #poems, interacting with each other as well as others, Gregor and I decided to create a new channel (#gregor). Since it only takes one to do this, he issued the actual **/join #gregor** command that created the new channel (none by that name had existed up to that time). Then I issued a **/leave #poems** command to exit my current domain, followed by a **/join #gregor** command in order to enter the new channel. This resulted in a new channel window named #gregor popping up on my screen.

Gregor and I went over to #gregor in order to talk in private for a while—not unlike behavior exhibited at a real party, where guests often migrate from populated rooms to sparser areas as moods shift. The following lines are taken from Gregor's log, not mine, since he was the one on two channels at once (that is, while I was only on the new channel #gregor, Gregor was still on #poems as well).

```
<Jayke:#poems> and deja vu two years ago
<Jayke:#poems> You won't have her! She is mine!
<Jayke:#poems> I won't let you take her from me
<Jayke:#poems> I will not lose her
<Jayke:#poems> She is all I have left, of me
<Jayke:#poems> of him
<Jayke:#poems> She does not cry.
<Jayke:#poems> --- 16 oct 94
<donrose> ever thought of being a screenwriter?! with your imagery
<Jayke:#poems> *end*
>yeah, I'd love to be a screenwriter
<donrose> do it!
>that would be awesome
<hawk:#poems> I like it.
<donrose> first i would get the best books on the subject
<Jayke:#poems> u understand it? :)
<hawk:#poems> But I think everyone else is asleep
<donrose> like Syd Field's trilogy
<donrose> including "Screenplay"
<donrose> and the sequel workbook
<hawk:#poems> As much as I understand anything this early
>I think I understand it... I like it... it's good
<Jayke:#poems> hm.. it was long.. did it take awfully long to get?
<donrose> it's like a how-to manual
<laurie:#poems> kept me guessing all the way through.. :-)
<hawk:#poems> not really
<Jayke:#poems> thanks greg
<Shmeck:#poems> there is something about reading poetry on irc...
the delay between lines...
```

```
>my firstname is Scott... if you're interested
>thanks
<donrose> youre welcome!
```

As the above log begins, Jayke is finishing up a poem on the #poems channel. Since the log was recording from the #gregor channel, inputs from other channels (e.g., #poems) are labeled with those channel names—plus the chatters' names, of course. As Jayke's poem ends, I am reacting to a previous poem of Gregor's (which he inputted earlier on the #gregor channel) by suggesting he try screenwriting too. From this point on, Gregor is both reading my advice about screenwriting and reading the comments that those on #poems are giving concerning Jayke's poem. He alternates between sending comments to #poems and talking to me on #gregor.

While this parallel processing is not an easy feat, it is doable. I doubt, however, that most folks could handle, say, 10 channels in parallel with any degree of enjoyment or efficiency (unless one happens to be *Star Trek*'s android Data).

For you the reader, I bet that tracking the above excerpt was not a piece of cake at first, especially if you're new to IRC. This would certainly be the case if you were actually on IRC and in the thick of things, having to read the above text the moment it comes in; it's a bit easier here because the log file is static history and we don't have to worry right now about taking part in any conversations. Still, at least you see now what this multitrack experience is like. Give it a try when you feel ready.

Moving On

If you've been reading the chapters straight through, you should have an idea about what sorts of things you can do on IRC, and how you can do them. But knowing *how* to do it something and how one *ought* to do it are sometimes two different matters. Things are pretty loose on the chat channels, but there are a few generally accepted rules of conduct you should be aware of if you want to make a good first impression. So in the next chapter we'll take a closer look at some of the finer points of IRC etiquette.

CYBERCHAT ETIQUETTE

What behaviors are prevalent on IRC, and how can one be sure that one's own behavior is "correct" more often than "wrong" or "questionable"? Although the line between right and wrong communication is often fuzzy, this chapter strives to provide a general guide to help you through the IRC manners maze.

In general, IRC tends to be more lenient of manners and behaviors that normally would be considered questionable in the real world. Perhaps this is true in part because widely utilized systems for multiuser chat are a relatively recent innovation on the Net, and hence are still "free form" and unrestricted compared to other Net domains like e-mail and USENET newsgroups.

Whatever the reason for the extra leeway on IRC, this could change as the number of Net users increases. More users means more points of view, which might slide the average opinion away from lenience and more towards restrictive ideas or intolerance. Although this could occur, I hope it will not; I believe the free and loose nature of IRC is one of its most attractive features. Since IRC (and the Net as a whole) has always tended to be self-correcting (i.e., those who do things "wrong" are quickly warned or even punished by other users), I expect the freedom of expression experienced on IRC to continue for some time.

Still, the need for a few generally accepted rules of conduct does exist, and will become even greater as the Net continues its explosive growth. We've touched on some of the most basic chat etiquette points in earlier chapters. But here we'll go into more depth, covering some rules of thumb for general IRC etiquette as well as advice on proper behaviors and expectations for the specific area of IRC-based virtual sex—what I call "sexchat." (Note: Some of the advice in this chapter is adapted from or inspired by the book *Minding Your Cybermanners on the Internet*, from Alpha Books—also written by yours truly.)

My 10 Commandments of Cyberchat Etiquette

Although this chapter provides a lot of advice, in this section I've boiled down the most important ideas into 10 "commandments" (depicted in their briefest form in Figure 5-1). Parts of these rules may have been stated in other forms by other IRCers, but together they constitute my own personal list of the of the 10 most essential. The other advice discussed later in the chapter is also important for users to know about, but the ideas contained in the following items seem to be mentioned the most by IRC gurus and server sites.

Be informed. Look, think and get the FAQs before diving in blind. This rule applies to any area of the Internet. Look before you leap, think before you type. It may be common sense, but it wouldn't be "common" if it weren't useful. Users of IRC form their opinions about you only by your actions and words, so always put your best virtual foot forward.

If you're a newbie to IRC, you might benefit from observing other users before jumping in with your two cents. For instance, you could lurk on channels, or access stored files of chat transcripts to learn the ropes. In addition, you might want to talk on existing channels before starting your own.

Pick a unique nickname. Using someone else's nickname is considered a big taboo on IRC. One reason for this is that having a unique name is one of the few things one can be relatively sure of in this virtual realm. Most IRCers want to feel somewhat certain that the nicks they pick can be associated with them for as long as they want.

Imagine if you tried to do business using the name IBM or Xerox. Those companies would almost certainly take actions to stop you, since they wouldn't want their goodwill, trust and name recognition to be handed to you by mistake. The same could be said for an IRCer who may have developed a good reputation and many online friends. In addition, having many users with the same name (whether it happened through accident or cunning) would just be plain confusing.

No verbose bots. In particular, don't do anything that could cause automatic flooding on channels. Flooding is quite annoying, to say the least, and violates the consensual reality that IRC depends upon. Imagine getting a slew of loud random noise or canned speeches over a conference (telephone) call and you'll get the general idea. Just because some clever computer whiz can create a bot to flood a channel with character strings doesn't mean it should be used. Playing around on one's own computer is one thing (and totally fine, in the libertarian view often found on IRC), but when

I. Be informed.
II. No same nickname.
III. No verbose bots.
IV. Respect server rules.
V. Respect channel rules.
VI. Respect operator decisions.
VII. If you dislike a channel, start anew.
VIII. Don't kick without an explanation.
IX. Don't hog bandwidth.
X. Avoid flame wars: tolerate intolerance.

Figure 5-1: *The 10 Commandments of Cyberchat Etiquette, in convenient tablet form.*

orked with millions of others the risk of inconvenience (or
ore critical. In fact, this rule is so important it often ap-
ome messages of many IRC servers.

nd that this rule does not mean all bots are bad. In
annels depend on them for smooth operation. One must
avoid the flooding variety. For example, if someone tells you to
use his or her cool new bot, and you don't understand the code behind
it or what exactly it will do in various scenarios, don't use it! Or at least
take steps to ensure it is not a flooding bot.

Respect a server's rules and requests. This should be easy to do, since
such rules are usually stated in the welcome message right after you
log into an IRC site. Many servers, for example, make the previous rule
of thumb (about flooding bots) into an outright bot ban. If you don't
agree with a server's rules or restrictions, you can try getting onto another IRC server.

Respect channel rules, regulations and expectations. When in cyberRome,
do as the cyberRomans do. For example, speak the channel's language
(e.g., don't type stuff in French on an all-Russian channel). And be re-
spectful of the intent of a channel. Folks using the #macintosh channel
would feel emotions ranging from surprise to outrage if someone initi-
ated explicit sexual acts on that channel. Knowing the topic of a channel helps in this regard, and is certainly the minimum awareness you
should have about any channel you intend to participate in. In general,
you probably should not join a channel if you're not planning on discussing the given topic. And if someone has already assigned a topic to
a channel, a good IRCer would not change it unless he or she had the
consensus of the entire channel.

Respect operator decisions. Channel operators rule—like it or not. Don't
be overly combative with an op. You should especially avoid excessive
arguing on a public channel. If you do, you could be kicked off a channel or even off IRC entirely. Think of joining a channel as getting your
driver's license, and the channel op as a state trooper.

If you don't like a channel, start a new one. Then *you* can rule (as chan. operator). Or let others rule; it's your choice if you are the creator. If being creator is too much pressure for you, jumping to a new channel can be as easy as switching to another that already exists. What would make a user want to leave one channel for another? For one thing, a crowded feeling (too many users on a channel) can irk some people. If a channel begins to feel pretty full—and overcrowding often happens when the world can gather at will—you could ask a few others on that channel to join you on another, particularly if you are not actively participating in any conversations on your current channel. If you decide to create a new channel, it could be a related spin-off, or have a totally different topic.

Don't kick someone off your channel without an explanation. This rule, which applies to channel operators, is an unwritten yet widely expected practice; IRCers are generally told why an op wants them off a channel. One of the reasons for this is so the "kicked party" can learn from any mistakes he or she has made.

Don't hog bandwidth. This can cover several circumstances. For example, don't talk on and on without letting anyone else get a word in edgewise (actually, others' words could still be seen on everyone's screen, but a non-stop talker's words would certainly monopolize it). And let others finish their thoughts (e.g., a poem in progress on the #poems channel, or an answer to someone's question—either of which may take several lines of "screen time"). No one likes to be interrupted.

Also, one should take lengthy or emotionally charged exchanges off of IRC. For instance, if you and one other IRCer insist on a long conversation, debate or electronic shouting match, IRC is no longer the best medium for you two; e-mail would be better. The overarching point here: IRC was invented for the purpose of *multi*user dialogue—so don't hog the Netwaves!

wars. Tolerate intolerance (and other points of view, in
 am writing this on Martin Luther King's birthday, this
 extra significance. IRC is often a democratic, some-
 ree-for-all, but most users learn to appreciate this,
 e sometimes say things that other people disagree with.
 Cers quickly learn to accept the idea that one must, at the very
 st, respect what some consider "alternative" points of view.

But what if one of these "alternative" views openly states that they
don't like *others'* points of view, or hate those that believe in them? This
is where tolerance comes in; if you give in to others' hateful feelings on
IRC, the situation can easily erupt into a flame war within one or more
channels (just as flaming can flare up over e-mail or USENET). In fact,
flames over IRC can be quite a bit "hotter" than on the other two areas
of the Net; because the flaming is in real time, there isn't the usual cool-
ing-off period that is built into e-mail and newsgroups.

The ideas behind this rule could be viewed as related to the ACLU's
reasoning when they supported a bigoted group's right to parade in
public (no matter how many citizens may have hated this display).
Freedom of speech is just as strongly defended in cyberspace as in real
space, if not more so; open and free communication means that some
people may try to use a medium for purposes you do not like. If so,
you can always ignore them ("change the channel")—or create other
cyberplaces for the expression of ideas you *do* believe in, so that IRCers
can have clear and easily accessible alternatives to the ideas you disap-
prove of. Remember, there are plenty of channels to go around on IRC.

Some Other Points of Protocol

Here are some additional rules of thumb relating to general IRC usage.
Some of these follow from the above "commandments," while others
cover different aspects of the IRC experience.

Don't try to access IRC without asking first. It is usually preferable to ask your system manager or administrator (sometimes called "sysadmin" or "oh great guru") before going to the trouble of finding, downloading and using an IRC client. This is because some managers do not want users participating in IRC activity, for various reasons (e.g., it can hog computer/network time away from other users, especially at peak usage hours).

If you do have a beef with a channel operator, work it out on a private channel or via e-mail. E-mail, for example, gives you time to calm down, formulate your thoughts more objectively, read it over and edit, even save the file and wait overnight to make sure it's the proper tone, and so on. Despite how wonderful IRC is, there are times when it's best to use another medium.

In general, keep language clean. Language should be kept clean on most public channels, as a default rule. (Sexually oriented channels are the usual exceptions.) Although it is rarer on the Internet than on commercial services' chat forums, you *can* be kicked off a channel if its operator dislikes your language and/or tone.

Conversation on private channels are exactly that—private—and hence most folks do not care what is said on these channels. If you find something offensive somewhere on IRC, or you yourself want to be more offensive than others on the channel care for, just take a tip from TV viewing and change the channel!

One hello/goodbye is enough. It's not necessary to greet everybody on a channel personally; one "hello" is usually sufficient, and the same goes for bidding farewell. Also, don't expect everybody to greet you back. On a large channel, greeting could produce a screenful of hellos. If you do want to greet someone, it is more considerate to the other users on the channel if you do it with a private message instead (e.g., using the /msg command).

Be forgiving of spelling and formatting oversights. After all, we don't worry about spelling and formatting when talking in real life; worrying about such details can slow down the conversational flow. Remember that cyberchat is meant to be informal and take place in quick bursts of ideas, like real chatting.

Don't impose PCness on an unPC area, or vice versa. Political correctness is revered on some channels and reviled on others. Act accordingly, and know thy audience.

Use a nickname that matches or highlights your personality. It's like wearing an outfit that shows your tastes. Remember, the text you choose to type is the only way you can make impressions over IRC.

Take all self-descriptions with a grain of salt. As in other areas of cyberspace, what you see or read may not be what you get. As the saying goes, "On the Internet, no one knows you're a dog." That is, you never really know who is on the other side of that nickname (in terms of sex, age, etc.). You should assume that some Netters, for various reasons, are experimenting (or actually living day-to-day online) with false personas—pseudonyms, fake IDs, that sort of thing.

You need not feel bashful asking questions about the sexual orientation of someone you are building a friendship or courtship with, especially if you're the type who must know someone's vital statistics right away. Or you can just revel in the ambiguity and rejoice that you can get to know someone without ever having to know their gender, age, race or other real world "trivialities." Besides, you might not get an answer—and even if you did, how would you know it was true?

Don't flame a cyberchatter you suspect of using a "false" persona. After all, taking on an artificial personality is one reason some folks cyberchat. In addition, who's to decide where the defining line between "real" and "fake" personas lies, whether online or in the real world?

Don't force an FTF (face-to-face) meeting if someone doesn't want one. Many Netters love cyberchat (either "clean" talk or sexual conversations) precisely because FTF meetings do not have to be a part of the process. Refusing an FTF meeting is *not* necessarily the same as rejection; some folks just want to keep everything virtual, even if they really like someone. Respect other IRCers' decisions—concerning FTFs or anything else. Also feel free to say you want to put off an FTF decision until later; some who really likes you will understand.

Make your channel title or topic clear enough to get its purpose and orientation across. A vague or misleading title can irritate unsuspecting visitors. For example, if you create a channel named #pictures, some IRCers could interpret this name as a hangout for discussion or exchange of sexually explicit pictures, while the true intent may be for discussion of computer graphics issues. (This kind of misunderstanding once happened for real.) So be as specific as you can when it comes to channel names and topics.

The Do's & Don'ts of Sexchat

If one applies a telephone culture metaphor to online interactions, one could predict that the popularity of phone sex numbers should carry over to a strong desire for Internet-based sex as well. Perhaps this accounts, at least in part, for the huge popularity of sexually oriented IRC channels like #netsex and #hottub, and the relatively large number of channels devoted to sexchat activities/topics.

Some folks feel that any form of virtual sex exhibits poor Net manners. However, for the large numbers of IRCers who accept the general principle, questions about manners are more complex. Some Netters just want to talk *about* sex; some of these people use IRC as their means to do so, but more often they use various USENET newsgroups for that purpose. Another class of IRCers want to *perform* actual virtual sex (no, that's not an oxymoron)—something the IRC medium is uniquely suited for. This section presents some etiquette advice for these daring folks. Keep in mind that many of the rules for general cyberchat presented above also apply to sexchat. Also keep in mind that portions of the following advice can be applied to general cyberchat. Although my compendium of advice is by no means exhaustive, it should be a good start for you sexchatters.

Type fast and write well. Some computer sex participants consider these qualities the online equivalent of physical attractiveness in the real world.

Learn how to spell. Bad spelling is a turnoff to some. And good spelling can be a turn-*on* to others (spelling fetish, anyone?).

Opening lines are extra important when meeting on IRC. Why? First of all, words are all you have to make an impression (no physical cues or breathy voice to compensate or augment). Second, chat channels can pop in and out of existence extremely fast, and people can move in and out of these "virtual rooms" just as quickly. Boredom will not be tolerated well in online sex, so get their attention fast!

Don't assume or flaunt a sexual orientation that doesn't fit the assumed orientation of the channel you're on. The more someone tries to emphasize a difference from the room's inhabitants, the ruder that person is acting. Proper etiquette suggests that this individual change to another room that better fits his or her needs. Or he/she can always start a new channel.

Balance sexual "goals" against the public chat etiquette guidelines given by your Internet service provider or system administrator. "Public" is the key word here. Since many chat channels are public, Netters hungry for more risqué sexual "action" might want to leave the public areas.

If you want to chat nonstop, free from "chatus interruptus," go private. Private channels can be created and are tailor made for this kind of activity. Dialogues in these private areas are confidential. However, it may sometimes be difficult to find out the correct way to get to the steamy private sex channels; you may need to know someone who can tell you how or invite you to join. Of course, this may actually help increase the anticipation (a lot of what sex is about, right?), and the ultimate pleasure when you do finally enter the hidden channels.

Don't reveal information that is meant to be private. If you have an understanding with one or more virtual "partners" to meet on a private channel, don't give out information about its participants or content, since the others in your group may assume that you'll all keep things secret. Letting the cat out of the bag violates their trust.

If you want to exchange images with content that may not be suitable for public consumption, use private messages or e-mail. In other words, don't do it in public.

Learn the proper "codespeak" used by denizens of the online sexspaces. For example, there are often codes used to tip off other users (on a public yet sexually explicit chat channel) that someone unwanted or uninvited may have entered. In general, it makes sense to act like one of the fold when you're trying to assimilate into a new world; you want to fit in as fast as possible, and "know the code" is a good mantra to repeat to yourself. Plus, it's just plain practical, since you won't fully understand what is being said and done without knowledge of the common slang and accepted actions of a particular channel.

When partaking in multiperson fantasy interactions, strive to maintain eroticism and consistency. That is, keep everyone in the mood, and don't ruin things by popping the "fantasy bubble." For instance, if person X says he or she is standing up, don't make an action that assumes he or she is sitting. Such events in effect shout "contradiction!," and may jar some of the participants, reminding them this is all just happening over phone lines with text-based personas. In other words, everyone assumes that everyone else is striving to maintain the consensual reality, so don't be the weak link in the cyberchain. Most important of all, don't whine and complain that cybersexchat is not really sex, or something like this. You're being a party pooper, and you'll probably get flamed royally as well.

Follow the rules and play the part for the channel you are having sexchat in. For example, some chatters might belong to a channel where it's assumed that you are buck naked while on that channel. Someone (e.g., the operator) might even claim that nudity is mandatory or you get kicked off the channel. Of course, you may wonder why this matters when it seems no one could prove whether you're really nude. But you should at least *act* as if you're nude.

It's generally considered acceptable to "swing" online, even if you're monogamous in the real world. After all, the fantasy element—being able to do online what some feel they can't do for real—is one of the main attractions of sexchat. And, of course, cybersex is safe sex.

However, using IRC channels with the goal of cheating for real is getting into the realm of bad taste, and getting out of the spirit of sexchat. Of course, all this should be adjusted for your personal point of view and moral system, and those of your virtual partner(s).

Moving On

Congratulations—you've made it through your crash course in IRC etiquette, and now you're sure to feel a new air of confidence as you surf through IRCspace. The only question remaining is, where on IRC will you go to try out your newly acquired social graces? There can be an overwhelming number of channels to choose from on IRC—hundreds, even thousands on most days (and you thought the much-hyped prediction of 500 TV channels was overkill!). To help you deal with all this choice and try to make sense of it, the next and final chapter provides an overview of several key IRC channels. It's a semi-organized smorgasbord of what IRCers generally believe are the most popular and interesting channels, plus those I feel are the coolest, strangest, most useful or most fun. You'll also find listings of many IRC-related resources available elsewhere on the Net, including FTP and Gopher sites, newsgroups and World Wide Web pages.

CHAT CHANNELS & RELATED RESOURCES

This chapter provides an overview of the range of IRC culture. Here you'll learn where and how to find the coolest hangouts and most informative IRC-related oases on the Net. More specifically, I'll be describing chat channels, USENET newsgroups that deal with IRC issues, World Wide Web pages that are dedicated to channels, and other useful IRC information.

Choice IRC Channels

The compendium in this section describes some prime channels on IRC (and/or the Undernet), out of a potential list of thousands. To get onto any of the channels listed, just use the /join command (e.g., /join #macintosh).

Wherever possible, I have grouped together channels with related themes. Most entries include a description of theme, and the longer descriptions are for channels that I find most interesting or most representative of IRC culture in general. Where no description is given, the subject matter should be self-explanatory—but if it's not, just leap onto that channel and find out for yourself. After all, that's half the fun of IRC!

Note that channels come and channels go. Some of those listed here may be gone when you try to join them. Others will have evolved into something different. There are no bouncers at the door of any channel, so usage patterns are not set in stone. In other words, a channel's name indicates only its *intended* theme or population mix. Short of kicking users off a channel, an operator cannot constantly control the talk in his or her domain. In other words, if you feel that chaos and entropy have a greater foothold on IRC than other areas of the Net, you're not far off!

If one of the chat areas listed here is unavailable when you attempt to join, try varying the spelling, capitalization, hyphenation, tense or other aspects of a channel's name. For instance, you might try a lowercase #initgame if you cannot find #Initgame, or try #mutualfunds instead of #mutualfund, etc. If this strategy doesn't work, try a different name with a similar theme (for example, #invest or #money instead of #mutualfunds). If you get onto a channel with a similar theme, you can always ask if the one you wanted truly exists. You may like the new one even better—ah, the joys of discovery!

Computers

#amiga
For users of Amiga computers.

#amigager
Short for Amiga German; this channel covers the same ground as #amiga, but in German.

#applellgs

Discussions for those still interested in this particular machine.

#c-64

Discussion of Commodore 64 computers (in case anyone is still a fanatic about them—get with the future, dude!).

#eu-opers

Designed for IRC sysadmins (server administrators) who are European (cute name, huh?).

#hack

Here you'll find hackers talking about one another or their accomplishments, for the most part. Of course, if you've always wanted to *pretend* to be a hacker or talk like one, here's your chance. (But don't tell anyone I recommended it! Hackers can be a very cliquish bunch.)

It may surprise you a bit that a group of folks who would seem to want secrecy and privacy seem willing to talk on a public channel. Perhaps this is an indirect way of reminding us that not all hacking is synonymous with wrongdoing or bad Netiquette. It also illustrates how IRC is still thought of by many as a fairly secret place to hang out and chat, since IRC is far from being the most known spot on the infobahn (for the average Net user, at least).

#Linux

About the POSIX-compliant PC operating system.

#macintosh

#macintosh is an open IRC channel to foster the discussion of the Macintosh platform and topics related to it. There is even a mailing list (called "poundmac-list") devoted to discussions of the #macintosh channel, so I guess you could say it is popular with IRCers! (Note, however, that this is a closed list and approval is granted only if the user has been on #macintosh for a significant amount of time.)

Take note: The IRCers who operate this channel warn new users that pirating is not tolerated on #macintosh; such an action by a user can result in him/her being kicked off (or even banned from) the channel. Even references to such acts that appear in your conversations can fall under their warning, so be careful!

#os/2

About IBM's OS/2 operating system.

#perl

About the Perl programming language.

#phreak

For phone phreaks (or phreakers) and hackers.

#root

System administrators hang out and discuss...well, administrating computer systems. You may want to resist the prankster's urge to ask a gardening question.

#unix

Chat focusing on the famed UNIX operating system often used on workstations (but not hugely popular on personal computers).

#www

Here is where one part of the Net (IRC) discusses another (the World Wide Web, and related topics such as Mosaic and Netscape, home pages, links, hypertext and so on). Traffic is bound to increase with the proliferation of WWW pages that discuss IRC. Channels are even spawning their own WWW pages, thereby broadening the community experience beyond the limits inherent in IRC's structure (for instance, WWW pages can and do display images of frequent channel participants, while IRC cannot as of this writing).

The Darker Side

Or you might prefer to call this category "The Other Side" meets "The Paranormal" meets "Freaky Stuff" meets "Gothic Ghoulish Guff."

#darkrealm

Discussions on things related to vampires and other horrors.

#gothic

Discussions about gothic stuff.

#vampire

Put your own "Interview With" joke here. If you want to stimulate debate, bring up Anne Rice or Tom Cruise. Or discuss any other aspect of vampire lore.

Film & Television

Some of the USENET newsgroups that discuss various TV shows are more frequented and have more consistently good content than the corresponding IRC channels. However, the real-time nature of IRC can't be beat for certain tasks—such as finding out what tonight's show is about when it's supposed to start in five minutes.

#disney

Chat about the Disney empire, in any of its manifestations (film, TV, animation, theme parks, software—the list is almost as long as the wait for Space Mountain).

#Klingon

It may sound like something you put in a dryer to stop static, but you Trekkers know better. Here you'll find discussions related to this race of Federation enemies-turned-allies.

#movies

You probably won't find any highly paid critics in the virtual aisles of this IRC space, but film discussions *are* the order of the day. Who knows, maybe some Netter practicing his or her critiques here will one day move on to other areas of the electronic frontier. But the ability to get many points of view at once and in rapid-fire succession is definitely unique to IRC—and probably will be for some time to come.

#startrek

Star Trek hasn't died yet, in over a quarter century of showings (some of the main characters have—but don't ask which ones on this channel unless you're wearing a flame-retardant uniform). New versions of the original series and a new planned film series keep the vision alive, as does this IRC channel. Trekkers are by definition a friendly, gregarious, social and global group, so #startrek was bound to form. Trek talk occurs here, and so does role playing, but you might want to lurk around a little before trying the latter.

#starwars

Geared for fans of *Star Wars*. George Lucas's sci-fi universe may have started with the films, but now the Empire encompasses books, software and more.

#twilight

Discussion of the *Twilight Zone* TV show. Note that this differs from #Twilight_Zone, which is an operator hangout and sometime help channel.

Games

#ad&d

Tune in here for role-playing as well as chat about Advanced Dungeons and Dragons.

#boggle

This channel was inspired by the word-discovery board game Boggle, popular among literate friends (now also an interactive TV game show hosted by Wink Martindale).

#conquest

Chat focusing on the fantasy game called Conquest.

#Initgame

Here's another IRC channel designed for relaxation and fun. An endless game of Initials is the order of the day here. One user at a time hosts the ongoing game, changing his or her nickname to a string of letters that stand for specific bits of information.

For example, in the nickname JL_MAAR, J and L represent the person's first and last name, the M is for male (F=female), the first A is for American (N=not), the second A is for Alive (D=dead) and R is for Real (F=fictional). Players enter abbreviated "questions" to which the host gives a simple Yes or No answer. For example, you could enter a set of jobs (abbreviated to a few letters) that the person in question may have engaged in. For instance, "TV flm" would get a "Yes," since TV was the right job area, and "Tlk" would get a "Yes," because my JL stands for talk show host Jay Leno. (Do the command /recap to get a summary of all information gathered so far in the game. The first user to guess right becomes the new host, and the game continues.)

#mtg

Chat about the game called "Magic: The Gathering."

#poker

Join this chat to find poker games continually in progress.

#RiskyBus

This channel is a virtual experiment of sorts, an attempt to add a bit of creative entropy and a dash of chaos to an established classic game show. The essence: this channel is an ongoing game of Jeopardy, where contestants enter questions to match given answers, just like on the real TV show. You can jump in and out at any time, playing as many rounds as you like. The game never ends.

Other elements unique to this IRC incarnation: There are no virtual buzzers; instead, the fastest typist to enter the correct question wins. Also, there's an automated online "robot" (referred to as RobBot) that runs things and requires players to precede each sentence with "Rob" so that it can recognize players' entries. On TV, the number of players is limited to 3; on IRC, the number varies, usually averaging about 30 at any given time.

Is this the future of game shows? Is RobBot more human than Alex Trebek? Is it a coincidence that all the letters in Pardo (as in announcer Don) are contained in the word "jeopardy"?! Try the #RiskyBus channel and see. (One tip: you may want to create a macro to automatically type "Rob" for you, to speed your typing!)

#studpoker

Stud poker is played here continually.

#truthdare

"An Adult Game of Truth or Dare" is the channel's own description of this IRC version of T-or-D, made popular in the wake of Madonna-mania. Although most people think of sex when this game's name is mentioned, it can actually involve a whole range of ideas and actions unrelated to sex; hence I consider it a general game. Still, to be fair, sex tends to dominate the subject matter on #truthdare. The game's fun to play or just watch.

Here's a refresher on the rules: When someone calls on you, you're asked "Truth or dare?" Answer "Truth," and you'll be given a question you are expected to answer truthfully. Answer "Dare," and you'll be given a task to complete. After your answer or completed dare, it's your turn to pick someone and ask them "Truth or dare?"

This channel seems the perfect forum for this game, with many users probably feeling less inhibited in their confessions and other verbal offerings than they would feel playing it face to face. Fun for those who don't think risqué is a four-letter word.

General Chat

Since IRC is generally a free-spirited, open-to-most-anything kind of place, it makes sense that some channels would have no specific theme at all. Here are some examples, places where general chat is the norm, where no topic is forced on you. Some of these, like #callahans, are like virtual reality versions of pubs, where you can hang out with the regulars.

#bored

The subject matter is general, but it leans toward the whining, bellyaching end of the chat spectrum. Many of those present here hang out regularly.

#callahans

Participants from USENET's alt.callahan newsgroup often hang out here. Wednesday evening is the usual gathering time, but you can go on other days as well (and note that by the time you read this, the meeting date may have changed). Perhaps you too will appreciate the friendly atmosphere and become a full-fledged "Callahanian." All topics are fair game, and Callahanians tend to be open with their feelings and experiences, good and bad.

#heart

Topics are general, but a large proportion of the participants are Taiwanese.

#heathers

Campy chat. The name comes from the cult film *Heathers* (a satiric early vehicle for Christian Slater and Winona Ryder).

#usa

Generic chatting goes on here, but it's mainly geared for folks in the United States.

Other Related Channels

#happy

#nicecafe

#silly

#talk

#talk2me

Hip Help Havens & Expert Enclaves

There may be several help-oriented channels on IRC at any time. Help channel names to try first are #help or #irchelp; others to try include #IRC_Prefect or #dead.

One channel *not* to seek help on is #Twilight_Zone, which wrongly has been labeled as an oasis for advice, perhaps because it is frequented by ops who might answer some questions when they feel like it. But don't hold your breath. As the World Wide Web reports on its #Twilight_Zone page, this "watering hole for operators and...hangers-on...still attracts a large number of operators and a coterie of fans," but "many of the regulars are short-tempered, sarcastic and often don't like being imposed upon." Channel access is often restricted, to boot—it might be secret, moderated, by invitation only, or all of the above—so you might wait until you feel more like an IRC guru before sauntering onto #Twilight_Zone.

Some advice: When asking for help on any channel, avoid prefacing questions with too many introductory remarks. IRC experts—and those who think they are—usually hate to waste time with wordiness. Just get right to what you want to say.

Meeting Places & Friendship Forums

Most IRCers are naturally friendly and outgoing—not surprising, since many are young, in college, free thinkers and willing to spend hours talking text-only to strangers. Hence, it is also not surprising that many meeting-oriented channels have been formed. These are ideal places for new users to start, as well as places where one can transform a stranger into a friend.

Although "cyberwhoopie" (or "the nano-nasty") may be in the minds and discussions of folks on these channels, the interaction tends to be more subtle than on the more sexually explicit channels discussed later in this chapter.

#cheers

This channel is a virtual bar, with a name inspired by the hit NBC TV show.

#40plus

A meeting place for for baby boomers and other groovy grokkers.

#hottub

Get virtually wet! This tub has a virtually unlimited capacity, so lose that towel and get in. This is one of the longest-running and most popular of IRC channels. It's almost always teeming with people. Other channels come and go, but there always seems to be a #hottub or #hottub2 or something similar around on IRC. Author and Internet expert Howard Rheingold has described #hottub as "an ongoing flirtation space...mostly heterosexual." You'll probably call it fun. You never know what the topic of conversation will be (which, of course, is pretty much what it's like when talking to others in a *real* hot tub). In fact, its popularity may be due to the fact that there are no built-in restrictions implied by the channel name, as there often are with other channels. Whatever the reason, jump on in.

#ircbar

The #ircbar is a virtual watering hole whose main feature is the Barman. He serves drinks, tells how to make more than 60 different cocktails and dispenses information on the operators. To learn more, type **/msg barman4 help** into IRC.

Of course, without real liquor you may not get real drunk—unless you count getting drunk on conversation, as many IRCers do. (In fact, there's a USENET newsgroup for recovering IRCoholics; see my entry on alt.irc.recovery in the "IRC-Related Newsgroups" section later.)

The #ircbar channel (you can also try #IRCBar or #IRCbar) has been going for more than a year and has gradually become more and more popular. People have requested to become operators. The channel and Barman have brought a lot of people together to form good friendships. And who knows; maybe we'll meet there, too!

#love

Here you'll find flirting and other general talk. Since teens often go to #teenlove, post-teens and adults might find more members of their own generation(s) here.

#penpals, #penpal

Making a new friend is one of the main goals here. The chat topics are often general. Response times are sometimes slow, but the talk is friendly.

#romance

Sounds all sweet and Manilowish, but cybersex is sometimes performed here, along with good, old-fashioned flirting.

#singles

Flirting is allowed. Being single helps, but (as they say on the Internet) who will know? (Lazy liars may appreciate that they don't need to hide that ring.)

#TahitiBar

A fun, mainly-Finnish hangout (at least Finnish seems to be spoken every time I visit it; see Figure 6-2 for a sample). However, this channel has spawned some nice World Wide Web home pages written in English as well as some Web pages in Finnish. The regulars on this channel plan regular, live (FTF) meetings, parties and other expeditions; some even contribute poetry. Is there a barmaid at #TahitiBar? Find out for yourself.

```
<Tai-Pan!taipan@lk-hp-11.hut.fi> kaupasta
<Tai-Pan!taipan@lk-hp-11.hut.fi> kuin
<Jaywalker!vwesterh@halinalle.cs.hut.fi> antaisin mita tahansa jos se palaisi
<Tai-Pan!taipan@lk-hp-11.hut.fi> kaupasta
<Tai-Pan!taipan@lk-hp-11.hut.fi> yleensa
<Jaywalker!vwesterh@halinalle.cs.hut.fi> anna stidit ja piikkarit niin kylla palaa
<Tai-Pan!taipan@lk-hp-11.hut.fi> 8 megalla
<Tai-Pan!taipan@lk-hp-11.hut.fi> muistia
<Tai-Pan!taipan@lk-hp-11.hut.fi> ja
<Tai-Pan!taipan@lk-hp-11.hut.fi> 500Mb kovalla
<ade!ade@pcuf.fi> tp, kylla ma tiedan etta pelkan pentiumin saa alle 10.000:lla mutta
ois se naytto siina kiva ja kovalevy ja vahan muistiakin =)
<Tai-Pan!taipan@lk-hp-11.hut.fi> ja 14/15" putkella
<ade!ade@pcuf.fi> ei saa
<Tai-Pan!taipan@lk-hp-11.hut.fi> KATSO HESARIAAAAAAA .. loppu .. avaimet aurinkoon
<ade!ade@pcuf.fi> TP, ei varmana saa... kerro mulle mista!
<sunic!whatever@tanipe.slip.jyu.fi> heheh....taa on hauskaa....(c:
<Tai-Pan!taipan@lk-hp-11.hut.fi> K-Kaupasta
<sunic!whatever@tanipe.slip.jyu.fi> hahaha
<Tai-Pan!taipan@lk-hp-11.hut.fi> ja ANttilasta
<Jaywalker!vwesterh@halinalle.cs.hut.fi> olen miehiston viihdytysryhman jasen 2
```

Figure 6-1: *Some sample dialogue (Finnish) from the #TahitiBar channel.*

#teenlove

The #teenlove chatspace features discussions about that awkward period in our lives when hormones rage and logic often takes a back seat.
If you are an experienced Netter, you might wonder how to identify the real teens on this channel. Just as teens may masquerade as older folk on #30plus or other channels, post-teens might make unannounced appearances on #teenlove. Remember, on IRC, and the Net in general, everything is not always what it seems.

#teens

All sorts of discussions for teens.

#30plus

Many IRCers recommend this channel for good times. It is mainly geared for those over 30, but don't be nonplussed if you're not 30-plus. Anyone is welcome. I have found this to be one of the friendliest of channels. If you do visit #30plus, say hi to Heloise (or "Hel"), the virtual den-mother denizen of this domain (and a sweet person who, along with other regulars, seems very willing to help new visitors to the over-30 channels). Hel mentioned that some of the participants even meet in person on occasion, face to face (or FTF to you Net-savvy abbreviation-lovers). If folks are willing to take this bold step (after all, most like the Net precisely because of its relatively anonymous interactions), you know it must be a friendly channel. Check it out.

#35plus

When too many folks are on #30plus, try this channel.

Music

#altmusic

Chatters talk about alternative music and sometimes venture into general chat.

#depeche

Join this channel to discuss the band Depeche Mode.

#guitar

Discussions revolving around this globally popular instrument and those who play or enjoy it.

#nin

Here, participants talk about the band Nine Inch Nails. Some use #nin to gather info about real-life hangouts where NIN-like (i.e., industrial) music is played.

#p/g!

The name is shorthand for Grace Under Pressure, and the channel is geared to fans of Rush (the band, not the stout talk show guy). Prepare for some Canadian jokes and some raunchy rants.

#pinkfloyd

Usually an international smattering of hard-core Pink Floyd fans.

#prince

Here's the place to discuss Paisley Park's pop star, Prince. (Or should I say, The Artist Formerly Known As Prince.)

#punk

You may have thunk punk stunk, but this form of rock music is definitely alive and well, and it's discussed here.

#rave

Buddy Holly may have popularized the term in the song "Rave On," but today's raves are a blend of techno brain-stim music, all-night marathon dancing and smart drinks. Sample snippets of rave talk here.

News

When there is breaking news, especially a crisis, the #report channel is likely to have the latest information available from IRCers around the globe. When active, #report has been called "better than the *New York*

Times" by some IRC observers, probably because it provides real-time, immediate feedback from real people, without mass-media filters and time lags, and because of the reputation this channel received after two 1991 crises (the Gulf War and Russian coup).

Note: If you cannot find the #report channel on IRC, try looking for the channel #discuss (remember, channels are not always forever on IRC, and may evolve over time with different names and participants). Or you could ask someone in a channel designed for IRC-related questions. You can also try searching for a channel name related to a recent news event. For example, after the earthquake in January 1995 that devastated the Japanese city of Kobe, the channel #kobe came into existence. On #kobe, people around the world communicated about the disaster and tried to coordinate help where possible.

If a late-breaking news story or major event involves a particular country or region of the world, try joining the channel that "specializes" in the affected country (see the "People, Places & Languages" section later in this chapter).

Opinions & Philosophies

These are channels where arguments abound. People may not always agree, but it's still heartening to see democracy in action.

#abortion

If you really think you can solve this issue over IRC, you're sadly mistaken, but at least it's a pseudo-safe environment, where people are armed only with words. Many folks have opinions locked in stone on this subject, but those who still have an open mind can wander in and listen to both sides here. But be careful; like any forum for charged issues, the flammability factor (i.e., the odds of getting flamed by other IRCers) is high.

#Anarchism

If I explained it, I wouldn't be very anarchistic, now would I?

#aynrand

The name is inspired by philosopher and writer Ayn Rand. This channel features debate about Libertarian ideas and more. Has been referred to as the "Objectivism Channel."

#Chomsky

"Noam Chomsky for President" is a common slogan here. Discussions center around this famed linguist and outspoken political activist.

#limbaugh

Rush Limbaugh stimulates debate, like him or not.

#Socialism

One of the last bastions around. Drab-colored shirts optional.

#veggies

Vegetarians of the world, unite! (Over a bowl of salad, perhaps.)

People, Places & Languages

There is a wide range of very popular channels devoted to various nationalities. Some of the most active are #England, #russian, #viet, #korea, #hk (Hong Kong), #taiwan and #tw, #aussies and #australia, #sweden, #germany, #francais and #francaise, and #europe (for that unified feeling). Some of these channels may not use English as the primary language, but if you get out a (recent!) globe and just jump in, it'll be the next best thing to a real world tour. (If I don't list any information for a channel, you can assume it is geared mainly toward those who speak or study that language, or who are from that country.)

#bawel

For Indonesians.

#beijing

Discussion may occur in Chinese or English, but the speakers mainly come from this Chinese city.

#canada

Intended for Canadians, but those who aren't from the Great White North hang out there too, eh.

#danmark

This is a Danish-themed channel. The language is mainly Danish, but the channel is open to all. Danish beer is a popular topic.

#England

#England has been a regular (i.e., nondisappearing) hangout on IRC for some time, and the people there tend to be friendly. In fact, the channel description states its subtitle as "The Friendly Channel [tm]." If they bothered to trademark such a name, they must be serious about being amiable! This channel has never just been for people from England; people all over the world meet here and become regular visitors to this virtual English channel (pun intended ;-).

#Esperanto

Dedicated to the Esperanto language, which was designed to be universal (or at least global). Do they actually speak Esperanto on that channel? Will Esperanto catch on like...well, the metric system? Visit this channel and see for yourself.

#42

A private channel version of #freenet.

#france

For French speakers, students and just plain Francophiles (but English is spoken at times, too).

#freenet, #kana

These are hangouts for Finnish speakers.

#gb, #GB

Also for those Britishers from (you guessed it) Great Britain.

#hk

This channel hosts mainly Cantonese speakers and Hong Kong students.

#hkfans

This chatspace is mainly geared for the Hong Kong student population.

#japan, #nippon

Geared for Japanese speakers.

#kampung, #malaysia, #warung, #penang

Malaysian-themed chat. On #penang, Malaysians often talk in English.

#latvia

For those from the former breakaway republic, now independent nation of Latvia. (For the geographically challenged, it's near Russia.)

#moscow

For Muscovites, Russians or those folks who just want to keep up with news from that region.

#newcastle

More specialized than #England; geared for folks from Newcastle—or those who love them. Natives are often referred to as "Geordies" (in case you are online and wonder why so many folks use that word). Since the dialect of this city has been described as "impenetrable," don't expect to fit like a glove right away—but given the friendliness of most Englanders I've met, it shouldn't take long. (Also, the impenetrability of many U.K. *accents* at least is not an issue in a text-based environment such as IRC.)

#polska

For conversation among Polish persons.

#russian

#russian is an IRC channel where Russians and non-Russians from around the world (or, if you prefer, Net) meet to chat and exchange news. #russian channel visitors include regulars from about a dozen countries including the U.S., Ukraine, Latvia and, of course, Russia. Most of these IRCers are either students or programmers (which is often true for other channels, too, since they often have more time and bandwidth access to the Net). Random chat is common on this channel, but serious discussion also takes place, especially between 22:00 and 24:00 EST—and, of course, during the occasional Russian coup or other crisis. Talk often ends on some other channel, since it is difficult to talk seriously in a sea of 20 to 30 virtual voices.

Although many #russian channel users speak English, one shouldn't be offended if asked to speak Russian, since many #russian regulars get tired of non-native languages. Finally, note that #russian is a relatively anarchistic channel; regulars claim that you can say anything you want, but anybody who doesn't like what you say can possibly kick you out. So, as on all channels with nationalistic themes, be careful out there!

#seattle

If you haven't already moved there (hear that, fellow Californians?), come talk about the land of coffee, grunge, Microsoft, Mount Rainier, rain (fittingly embedded in the previous mountain name) and Bill Nye the Science Guy.

#seoul, #korea

Mostly for Korean speakers and students.

#siam

Thailand-oriented, but the words may be in either Thai or English.

#tibet

This is where Tibetan issues are discussed. You don't have to be from this land. You need only be interested in the culture in some way. Here's one place where the Tibetans can at least be free of physical persecution. Related channel: #buddhist.

#tw

For Taiwanese folks. English is used for many discussions.

#viet, #vietnight

Vietnamese speakers' forum.

Other Related Channels

#asian	#israel
#Bosnia	#italia
#boston	#japan
#brasil	#kuwait
#china	#laos
#chinese	#london
#colombia	#melbourne
#dutch	#norway
#egypt	#pakistan
#espanol	#palestine
#filipino	#singapore
#florida	#Slovenia
#hmong	#Sweden
#iceland	#taipei
#india	#texas
#iran	#turks
#ireland	#Wales

Philosophy, Religion & New Age

#biblestud

That's "stud" as in "study" or "student"; religious discussion of biblical topics.

#buddhist

Discussion of the Buddhist religion or philosophy (some argue over which it is—but remember that it doesn't really matter, it's the result that counts). Related channel: #tibet.

#christ

Discussion of Christian issues.

#christian

Same topic as #christ; any of the various Christian denominations may be the focus of discussion.

#islam

Discussions related to this globally popular and rapidly growing religious faith.

#jesus

The talk is supposedly about Christ, but this is not always the case on this channel. Although the channel name indicates a very serious tone, some users recommend a sense of humor.

#tibet

See review under "People, Places & Languages."

#wicca

For those who are into Wicca (some call it witchcraft).

Poetry

On the #poems channel, poems are made online, before your eyes, and criticism is usually immediate. If you always wanted to be a creator, listener and critic all at once, here's a great experimental ground to do so. I loved creating a "collaborative improvised" poem with someone I'd never met before. Then others joined in with lines of their own! Truly an experience unique to IRC. You gotta try it.

Although you can find poems in progress here, even completed ones, it is often great fun to watch things degenerate into nonpoetic drivel. Still, the occasional good poem is worth the effort to check out this channel—and, if they're poor, you'll feel that much better about your own "magnum opus." (Another plus is that that the people are friendlier on this channel than on many other IRC channels.) At the time of this writing, a poetry contest was also planned.

Science & Science Fiction

#astronomy

Try this if you're into stars and heavenly bodies that don't reside in Hollywood.

#Klingon

See review under "Film & Television."

#startrek

See review under "Film & Television."

#starwars

See review under "Film & Television."

#twilight

See review under "Film & Television."

Sex

Like it or not, it gets down and dirty on many of these channels, so be forewarned. But for those in the right frame of mind, these channels can be liberating and stimulating and the risks (at least those of the physical kind) are nil. These are among the most popular of the IRC channels. Given life in the '90s—and the fact that most IRC users are young, in school or acting as if they were—it's not hard to figure out why.

#bdsm

The name is short for bondage, discipline, sado-masochism. Open to all, but designed for those really into this stuff; if you lurk or act uncool or don't participate, you'll likely be shut out or booted off. When the channel is not used for virtual activity, it's often devoted to discussion of rights and one's personal space. There are even bots on this channel, appropriately named Hanki and Panki; explore them for yourself. Or, if you're not so daring, try the command **/msg panki dcchelp**.

#bondage

Same basic idea as #bdsm, but by invitation only.

#crossdres

Private channel dedicated to transvestites, or even lovers of *Rocky Horror.* Probably has seen increased traffic since the release of the film *Priscilla, Queen of the Desert.*

#erotica, #kink, #sex, #wetsex

General sexchat and action (but remember: on IRC, action doesn't speak louder than words).

#hotsex

This channel offers general chat about sex (plus flirting) that is not always scorching hot (#netsex seems to top it at times).

#hottub

See review under "Meeting Places & Friendship Forums."

#netsex

Do I really need to describe this channel, folks? Suffice it to say, #netsex is the granddaddy of IRC sex channels. Many people are much more forward on this channel than in real life, and you should be ready to hear (via text, of course) just about anything.

#phonesex

Seems to me that any sex on IRC is essentially the same as phone sex, just via text instead of voice (in a sense you are even using a phone, since your modem dials and uses a phone line).

#spanking

If I have to explain this, you deserve one.

#truthdare

See review under "Games."

Sex: Gay/Bi Themes

#bisex
For bisexuals.

#gam
Intended for gay Asian males and their partners.

#gaysex
Discussions about gay sex, and occasional text-based (virtual) activity.

#gaysm
Gay S&M chat and activity.

#lesbos
Lesbian chat and activity.

Sports

#cricket
For lovers of this sport. The users are mainly European, but all are welcome, mate.

#karate, #martial-a
For lovers of the sport/exercise/way-of-life/philosophy of karate and the martial arts.

#nba
Love basketball? Then dunk yourself here for a discussion of the National Basketball Association or things related to it.

#soccer

Discussion about the most popular spectator sport in the world.

Support Groups

The #12step channel is the IRC analog to the traditional 12-step recovery meetings that occur in the real world. Who knows, maybe Stuart Smalley will show up! Current meeting time is Sunday night (for those in the U.S. time zones, at least).

Video Games

#doom

This channel is a cousin of #vidgames (see below) but goes into more detail about one particular game—you guessed it, Doom. On #doom, you can meet other players of this wildly popular (some say addictive) game. And some players use it to find others who have the Internet Head-to-Head Daemon (IHHD) software, which lets folks play Doom over the Net. (Note: Some "Doomers" may want to try finding the #modemdoom channel if #doom is not active for some reason.)

Related channels include #falcon3.0 and #bolo, where aspects of these other games are discussed by their respective fanatics (I mean, players). And now that Doom II is being released, don't be surprised if a #doomII channel begins taking up IRC bandwidth sometime in the near future.

#vidgames

Join this channel for a discussion of topics related to videogames past, present and future. Some may use #vidgames to brag about high scores, and others might rebut in kind. Or IRCers might ponder puzzles they or others have found in games (especially newer ones) or discuss other problems. Still others might bring up hidden gems and surprises to be found in certain games (especially older ones). Even the possible rise of virtual reality as the new game paradigm has been discussed here.

Undernet Channels

Some "regular" IRC channels have analogous counterparts on the Undernet—that is, you can try using the same name, like #IRCbar, with a different spelling. However, there are also some channels unique to the Undernet, and this is one reason it's worth your while to visit this alternate chat universe.

One very intriguing channel unique to the Undernet is #Podium, the site of a meeting of minds called the Internet Roundtable. Some call it a cyberspace talk show. Well-known writers and thinkers (famous, at least, to Net regulars and media mavens) stop by periodically to talk with one another as well as with IRCers visiting #Podium. (The default time has been 10 p.m. EST.) The question and answer part of the show is typically indicated by the show/meeting host about 10 to 15 minutes after the show begins. During Q&A, channel visitors can put their two cents in via the /msg command. For example,

```
/msg #QUESTION What will the Internet look like by 2001?
```

For more information about the Internet Roundtable speaker series, see the "IRC-Related Gopher Sites" section later in this chapter. Perhaps the advent of more of these intelligent chat channels, plus other innovative uses of worldwide chat yet to come, will counterbalance some of the noise/garbage that takes place on so many other channels (IMHO, as well as the opinions of many other IRC users). This may one day be seen as analogous to the alternative that PBS and cable TV provided to the television programming that preceded their arrival.

See Appendix A for an alphabetized list, plus brief descriptions, of some other Undernet channels. The number and diversity of channels and users is not yet as great as on "regular" IRC, but some consider that an advantage.

IRC-Related Newsgroups

Now that I have listed some favorite channels, let me list some other IRC-related places to visit on the Net. Our first destination is newsgroups that discuss IRC issues. You can learn a lot about chat-related issues by rummaging around in these groups, which have been proliferating on USENET. Other newsgroups may help Netchatters too, but those listed here are more geared to the concerns of new IRC users. For access to most if not all of the groups, you might look at the Gopher site gopher.msu.edu.

alt.irc

If you really love IRC, you can use alt.irc as an asynchronous (non-real-time) channel with IRC itself as the topic. Here is a place to further foster the spirit of online community that starts with the IRC channels. Of course, things can progress in the opposite direction, too—people may meet on IRC, get an idea for a new channel or want to talk more in real-time mode, and hence go to IRC to continue conversing. And if you are *really* addicted to IRC, try the alt.irc.recovery newsgroup instead.

alt.irc.ircii

Discussions about the ircII client, one of the oldest. This newsgroup is popular with UNIX folks, who are the main users of ircII. However, with the advent of newer clients (such as the more graphical and intuitive programs, like Homer for the Mac), it shouldn't be long before other client-specific newsgroups appear on USENET.

alt.irc.recovery

Here's a haven for those recovering from IRC addiction. Addicts past and present may pop in. Many IRC users admit that overuse leads to feelings of isolation and/or less time spent with loved ones and friends in the real world. This newsgroup serves a function not unlike an on-line AA meeting. Substitute the term IRCoholics for Alcoholics, and you get the idea. Addicts and recovering addicts give support, testimonials and advice, and engage in debates. And if someone wants to learn how to avoid becoming an IRC addict in the first place, alt.irc.recovery can be useful as well.

Other Related Newsgroups

alt.irc.announce: Announcements of interest to IRCers.

alt.irc.bot: On the creation of IRC bots.

alt.irc.corruption: About the darker side of IRC.

alt.irc.hottub: More talk about this popular channel.

alt.irc.lamers: About IRC folks who are considered unhip.

alt.irc.opers: For IRC operators.

alt.irc.ops: Also for IRC operators.

alt.irc.questions: To get help; a newbie oasis.

alt.irc.sleaze: Covers more dark-side stuff and flamage.

alt.irc.undernet: About Undernet, the mirror IRC system.

news.answers: Where you may get answers to IRC queries.

Channel-Related WWW Pages

Some IRC channels are so popular they have expanded onto the World Wide Web as well. Below I discuss some channels that have associated home pages on the Web. Some of the things you may find on these "channel pages" include general information about the channel; lists of regular visitors' real names, e-mail addresses and/or nicknames (so you can identify them on IRC); digitized images of some visitors; sample dialogue from a previously stored session log or a "channel mirror" (showing the last few lines that were said on the channel—hence it's almost real-time); descriptions of past channel-related events; info about upcoming live (FTF) parties for channel regulars; links to other IRC-related information; and links that let you telnet to IRC itself. Pages rarely contain *all* of these things, but most provide a good subset. If you have WWW access, I highly recommend that new IRC users check out these pages *before* going onto the actual corresponding channels. It never hurts to prepare!

#England

The Friendly Channel [tm]

#England is a regular <u>channel</u> on <u>IRC</u> and people there are generaly very friendly. This channel has never just been for people from England, people all over the world meet here.

Will add small gifs for all I can find in near future, don't worry.

People regular (or used to be regular) on this channel:

- Anniee bsa044@cent1.lancs.ac.uk
- AnneMarij end010@cent1.lancs.ac.uk

Figure 6-2: *The #England home page on the WWW.*

#England

Like a growing number of IRC channels, the #England channel now has a WWW page where channel enthusiasts can find a list of common visitors to #England on IRC, as well as a growing collection of picture files (gifs) of channel users. In effect, such WWW pages expand the community feeling that IRC channels often foster, and #England's does the job very well. (In fact, some call it the best IRC-channel-related Web page yet constructed; try it for yourself and see.)

URL: **http://www.fer.uni-lj.si/~iztok/england.html**

#hottub

It's such a popular channel, it just had to spawn this "Web tub."

URL: **http://www.ora.com:8080/arsenio/hottub/**

IRC Channels

This page provides links to some of the more widely visited channel-related home pages. However, an even bigger list, with more annotation, can be found within the IRC-Related Documents page (see under "General IRC-Related WWW Pages" below).

URL: **http://www.funet.fi:80/~irc/channels.html**

#macintosh

If you like the #macintosh channel, here's an official #macintosh home page. It offers these examples of common channel topics:

- Cmon baby...set my Intel-based PC on fire!

- Just because a binary is -fat- doesn't mean it doesn't work.

- Promote global warming! Save on heating costs! Buy a Pentium.

- I want my PowerPC!

Since we all know technology changes at blinding speed, I'm sure the topicality of these topics won't last long!

URL: **http://disserv.stu.umn.edu/~thingles/ PoundMac/**

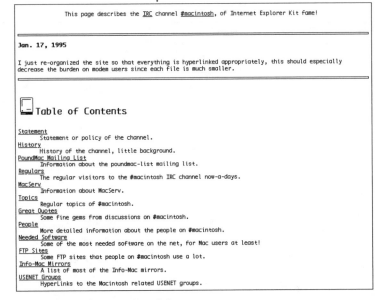

Figure 6-3: *The #macintosh home page.*

#russian

According to the #russian WWW home page, this channel is not just used for chatting and news updates, but also to "kick each other's butt." Despite (or perhaps because of) this fact, the #russian home page is one of the most complete in listing details about frequent visitors to the channel. Other items contained in this page include a general description of the channel and its rules, pictures of #russian regulars, an FTP link to an ircII client, and even information about a bot named "BSDBabe."

Another passage from this page (presumably written by a Russian): "Unfortunately for some of us [and fortunately for others]...citizens of the former USSR are scattered around the world and some of them who knew each other before need visas and other bureaucratic s**t to meet each other in person. Thus, #russian is the only way for such people to converse with their relatives and friends who may live in hundreds of kilometers from them." Yet another ringing endorsement for IRC's power and usefulness.

URL: **http://www.cs.umd.edu/users/fms/ RussianIRC.html**

#Sweden, #Danmark

IRC was invented by a man from Finland, so it's only natural that Scandinavians are among the more avid users of Internet chat. Their IRC inter-

---

The #Sweden IRC Channel

We're just a bunch of people who apparently have too much time that we don't know what to do with, and thus waste on IRC, discussing life, the universe, and everyting. When left alone we speak Swedish, but we can usually be persuaded into English. There are occasional outbreaks of other languages too, but that's generally frowned upon by the ones who don't speak that particular language.

You may want to check out the FTP archive at gwaihir.dd.chalmers.se where you can find, among other things, IRC-related software and pictures of some of us.

(Probably of Swedish interest only) Om man ska prata svenska är det kul om man kan skriva åäö rätt. Jag har satt ihop lite tips om hur man får det att fungera.

Talking electronically is fine, but it's nice to meet people face to face once in a while too. There's a party planned for mid-january 1995, in Linköping, for this purpose.

#Sweden Regulars With WWW Home Pages

- Ace Adam Rappner
- Al-X Alexander Foborg
- Cheese Magnus Östvall
- Crab Micke Nyström
- cybbe Per Wikman
- Danni Daniel Nilsson
- Darkface Patrik Olsson
- DoctorWho Roffe Larsson
- Dsoul8 Jörgen Persson
- Englund Patrik Englund
- Flognat Andy Eskilsson
- Fredde Fredrik Jagenheim
- guff Fredrik Gustavsson
- Guran Mikael Kaivo-oja
- Hyler Martin Hylerstedt
- Ille Christian Fredriksson
- Iorlas Magnus Lundgren
- Jed Johan Edbäck
- jonTe Jonas Ahrentorp
- Kattis Kathleen Trujillo
- levitte Richard Levitte (not so regular)

Figure 6-4: *The #Sweden home page.*

actions often extend to real life, and Web pages are an ideal way for Scandinavians or other IRCers to exchange information about such "extra-IRC activities."

URL for Sweden page: **http://www.lysator.liu.se/ ~ture/irc-sweden.html**

URL for Danmark page: **http:// www.daimi.aau.dk/~bde/irc-danmark**

#TahitiBar

There's a lot of useful information, as well as neat features and graphics, on this page and the pages that it links to. (Note: Since the dialogue on the #TahitiBar channel is often in Finnish, one could think of this page as a kind of unofficial Finnish home page.)

URL: **http://matserver.math.jyu.fi/tahitibar/ bar.html**

#unix

UNIX people will find useful stuff here, including a list of #unix channel regulars, as well as links to additional pages of interest.

URL: **http://www.seas.upenn.edu/ ~mengwong/irc.unix.html**

 Official #TahitiBar Homepage

Hello My Friend and Welcome to the Legendary TahitiBar!

For a layman **#TahitiBar** is just another <u>IRC</u> (<u>IRC-opas</u> in Finnish) channel but there is more to it than meets the eye. **#TahitiBar** is a channel with a <u>History</u>, Mission, lots of merry <u>customers</u> (with <u>pictures</u> and <u>homepages</u>) and last but definitely not least there is also a <u>barmaid</u> there.

#TahitiBar has also expanded outside the Net, most of the regulars in the channel know each other in real life too and <u>The First Official Annual Jyväskylä IRC Beach Party</u> was held july 27 1994. In short, **#TahitiBar** is an excellent channel, should I say one of the best (Who cares about modesty??:-)), and a very good place to spend your leisure time, so why not give it a try and <u>join</u> us all there!

Push

(#TahitiBar says Hello! to Catharine "CAT" Evans @ <u>mcom.com</u>)

 Not So Interactive #TahitiBar

IF you don't have a IRC-client near you right now you can check what is happening in the Bar today. Just follow this link to the <u>#TahitiBar WWW-mirror.</u> There you can see lates 20 lines from the legendary **#TahitiBar.**

Figure 6-5: *The #TahitiBar home page.*

General IRC-Related WWW Pages

Big Dummy's Guide to the Internet

Information that includes IRC, but goes beyond it to related topics (such as MUDs, which are similar to channels but have story/narrative elements and often more bots).

URL: **http://www.hcc.hawaii.edu/bdgtti/bdgtti-1.02_15.html**

IRC Connections

Links to IRC via telnet (in lieu of using your own IRC client).

URL: **http://alpha.acast.nova.edu/irc/connect.html**

IRC Frequently Asked Questions

It's always good chat etiquette to get the FAQs.

URL: **http://www.kei.com/irc.html**

IRC Home Page at Funet, Finland

An informational page located at the birthplace of IRC.

URL: **http://www.funet.fi:80/~irc/**

IRC-Related Resources

Lots of assorted information here, featuring links to resources all over the Net. Examples include text documents pertaining to IRC, pictures of IRCers, Web pages built by IRCers,

---

```
IRC - Internet Relay Chat
                 ▲

IRC is world wide network for interactive chatting over Internet. There are pointers
to different IRC related documents below.

  ● Documentation for protocol and usage.
  ● How to connect to IRC.
  ● IRC software (clients & server) by anonymous ftp.
  ● Pictures of people who use IRC
  ● Some well-known channels in IRC.
  _____

  irc@irc.funet.fi
```

Figure 6-6: *The IRC home page at Funet, Finland.*

IRC-related newsgroups, mailing lists, FTP and Gopher sites and even Undernet information. Also has a nice collection of links to channel-related home pages.

URL: **http: //urth.acsu.buffalo.edu/irc/WWW/ircdocs.html**

Other Related WWW Pages

These contain or point to (you guessed it) more useful IRC information:

URL: **http://coombs.anu.edu.au/pub/irc/**

URL: **http://alpha.acast.nova.edu/irc/**

URL: **http://eru.dd.chalmers.se/home/f88jl/Irc/ircdocs.html**

URL: **http://www.enst.fr/~pioch/IRC/IRC.html**

URL: **http://irc.informatik.uni-oldenburg.de:8081/~ircadm/**

Undernet-Related WWW Pages

Aaron's IRC page

A small Undernet-related page.

URL: **http://sci.dixie.edu/~agifford/undernet/**

```
IRC Related Resources on the Internet

Version 2.1.7 by pjg

from

Version 2.1.6 by ricks

Contents:

    • Introduction to this document
    • What's new
    • Documents
        ○ General purpose (primer, faq, manual, ...)
        ○ Reference material - IRC protocol
        ○ Policy and Administration
        ○ Sociology and Psychology
        ○ IRCII scripting
        ○ Misc documents - Look here !
    • Misc resources
        ○ IRC channels with WWW pages
        ○ Connecting to IRC via telnet
        ○ Pictures of IRC users
        ○ Meta list of other IRC users' home pages
        ○ Logs from big events
    • Other sources of information
        ○ Other good hypertext IRC pages
        ○ IRC related newsgroups
        ○ IRC related mailing lists
        ○ IRC related ftp sites
        ○ IRC related gopher sites
        ○ Undernet hints


Introduction

This is a summary of IRC related resources on the net. It is, by no means,
comprehensive, and you might find newer material at other places. I am, however,
confident that this is the most complete reference collection for information
regarding IRC. If you have additional documents, or find outdated material here,
please email me (f88jl@dd.chalmers.se) the necessary information to correct it.
Any suggestions, complaints or comments are welcome.

Contents
```

Figure 6-7: *A page providing links to many IRC-related resources*

Joker/Mailer's IRC page

Undernet-oriented information, in French.

URL: **http://esquilino.enserb.u-bordeaux.fr:8001/TOP/irc/index.html**

The Undernet

A page containing a short introduction to the Undernet, with links to more Undernet documents.

URL: **http://http2.brunel.ac.uk:8080/~cs93jtl/Undernet.html**

Undernet IRC Faq

URL: **http://sci.dixie.edu/~agifford/undernet/underfaq/index.html**

IRC-Related FTP Sites

Want to read archived logs of conversations that show how others have used IRC? (Or relive crises, from wars to coups to earthquakes in Los Angeles?) Then do that anonymous FTP thing at the locations listed below. The address for each site is given in URL (Uniform Resource Locator) format. If you do not use Mosaic, Netscape or another Web browser for your FTP access, use only those parts of the address that are applicable to your software client.

Gulf War IRC Logs

The 1991 Gulf War was arguably the first widely publicized event to show off IRC's special abilities. The Gulf War IRC log site (at the location described below) is where you can read, among other things

- "Official" Desert Storm logs from the #report channel.

- The granddaddy log of Jan 17, 1991, from the #peace channel.

- A transcript of IRC discussions about the bombing of Israel.

These logs are not just interesting for historians of real life; they are also useful for historians of the Internet and IRC itself. They illustrate perfectly how people use IRC, even come to depend on it, for up-to-the-nanosecond news. And the logs are just plain fascinating, like entries from scores of interwoven diaries, all being written simultaneously during stressful times.

URL: **ftp://sunsite.unc.edu/pub/academic/communications/logs/ Gulf-War/**

IRC Frequently Asked Questions

In addition to the Web location given earlier, the IRC FAQ can also be found at the following FTP site:

URL: **ftp://cs.bu.edu/irc/support/alt-irc-faq**

IRC Primer

Most IRCers in the know say the best basic IRC user's manual to access is the IRC Primer. It's available in plain text, PostScript and LaTeX. You can download an IRC Primer from various sites, including the following:

URL: **ftp://cs.bu.edu/irc/support/**

URL: **ftp://nic.funet.fi/pub/Unix/irc/docs/**

URL: **ftp://coombs.anu.edu.au/pub/irc/docs/**

IRC Tutorials

Another good place for basic IRC information is the IRC tutorials. There are three documents: tutorial.1, tutorial.2 and tutorial.3. The third tutorial mentions a fourth, which hopefully will be released by the time you read this.

URL: **ftp://cs-ftp.bu.edu/irc/support/tutorial.***

Russian Coup IRC Log

At least as fascinating as the Gulf War logs, the IRC report documenting the 1991 Russian coup (or the tumultuous trek of Gorbachev, if you prefer) is the other document many feel is the earliest, best showcase of the power and benefits of IRC. The IRC log site related to the coup events (at the location described below) lets you relive, in often scary detail, the fear and ultimate determination of the Russian people. You can track the shift in discussion tone over time: transforming from confusion and fear to resolve and finally to relief as the crisis fades.

URL: **ftp://sunsite.unc.edu/pub/academic/communications/logs/ report-ussr-gorbatchev**

Other Related FTP Sites

Those looking for more technical information can get the IRC RFC (rfc1459), available at all RFC FTP sites as well as the following location:

URL: **ftp://cs-ftp.bu.edu/irc/support/rfc1459.txt**

To access the main Undernet distribution site, go to this address:

URL: **ftp://undernet.org/undernet**

Various IRC-related material is available at this site:

URL: **ftp://sunsite.unc.edu/pub/academic/communications/irc/**

IRC-Related Gopher Sites

Following are Gopher sites where you can find IRC-related information. The address for each site is given in URL (Uniform Resource Locator) format. If you do not use Mosaic, Netscape or another Web browser for your Gopher access, use only those parts of the address that are applicable to your software client.

gopher.it.lut.fi

This Gopher site contains some interesting documents, but many recommend the World Wide Web version instead.

URL: **gopher://gopher.it.lut.fi/11/net/irc**

URL: **http://www.it.lut.fi/1/net/irc**

gopher.nvg.unit.no

Here you'll find some scripts, pictures of Norwegian users and IRC poetry.

URL: **gopher://gopher.nvg.unit.no:70/11/IRC**

Internet Roundtable Society

General information about the Internet Roundtable Society speaker series and details about participating in Internet Roundtable meetings can be found respectively in the following sites:

URL: **gopher://199.4.107.1:150/00c%3A/whatis/whatwedo.txt**

URL: **gopher://199.4.107.1:150/00c%3A/whatis/howtable.txt**

```
What we do

These sections are roughly written and still under construction.
Please bear with our dust. Thanks!

The Internet Roundtable Society's purpose is to provide our
members with:

  - direct access to important people in our society:
    newsmakers, authors, people with fresh ideas, people who are
    making a difference

  - exposure to all viewpoints, so that they can make informed
    decisions

  - the resources to make a difference

    Our members are an online community of bright, involved men
and women who enjoy stimulating discussions on a wide variety
of topics.  Each week the Society invites authors, policy
makers, and other interesting people to share their insights
with our members, at the Internet Roundtable.

    Roundtables are live, online, interview talk shows at which
members can chat with interesting people about intriguing
subjects.  The Roundtables are professionally produced, high
quality, and fast paced.

All Roundtables begin at 10:00pm EDT (7:00pm PDT).
Some of our guests include:

Frances Moore Lappe' and Paul Martin Du Bois,
Co-Directors of the Center for Living Democracy, and co-authors of
The Quickening of America.  Frances Moore Lappe' is widely known
for her book, Diet for a Small Planet.  Coming November 2 with host
Kevin Pursglove

Ann J. Simonton, activist and founder of Media Watch.
Coming November 9 with host Kevin Pursglove

Susan Stamberg, "the first lady of radio" - Special Correspondent to
NPR and former host of "All Things Considered" and "Weekend
Edition / Sunday".  Stamberg is the author of two books, and co-editor
of a third.  "TALK: NPR's Susan Stamberg Considers All Things"
chronicles her two decades with NPR.
Coming November 16 with host Kevin Pursglove.

Anne Lamott, author of "Operating Instructions", and her most recent
work, "Bird by Bird".  Coming Tuesday, November 22 with guest host
Sedge Thomson.

Howard Rheingold, Author of "The Virtual Community", and editor of "The
Millennium Whole Earth Catalog".  Coming December 7 with host  Kevin
Pursglove.
```

Figure 6-8: *About the Internet Roundtable Society.*

IRC-Related Mailing Lists

For tech weenies, operlist is a list that discusses current (and past) server code, routing and protocol. You can join by e-mailing operlist-request@kei.com.

Another mailing list, ircd-three@kei.com, exists to discuss protocol revisions for the 3.0 release of the ircd. Send e-mail to ircd-three-request@kei.com to be added to this list.

Moving On

Congratulations—you've made it through all the chapters in this book! Now you should have a pretty good idea what you can do on IRC, how to do it, and where to find information related to chatting online. Before you close this book, however, you might want to check out the pages that follow, or periodically seek out these areas as you delve deeper into IRC. They provide still more useful bits of information to help you—including lists of servers and channels, a glossary of terms, and a bibliography of related reading material.

What does the future hold for IRC? Of course, no one knows for sure, but there are some general trends. First, much of the Internet is heading toward more incorporation of graphics, audio and video in addition to text, so IRC will probably begin to add more of these elements as well. This is already happening to a limited degree, as many regular IRCers have put their images online (see some of the channel-related Web pages).

In a few years, IRC may give you the choice to accompany your channel dialogue itself with still pictures or even video (of you or of something else), as well as some kind of audio. You may be able to choose between text and voice for both input and output. Plus, the interaction between you and your client about these and other preferences might itself take place in a more user-friendly fashion (e.g., via a spoken exchange with a client that seems more like an online personality than a faceless, voiceless program). The bottom line: There should be a much richer level of interaction on IRC in the future than there is now. Some users may embrace this new multimedia environment, while others might cherish and preserve today's "good old-fashioned" text-only IRC.

Maybe I'll see you on IRC. Hint: I'm often on #30plus and #macintosh, but I'll leave it as a challenging exercise for you to try to figure out my nickname, if and when you think you've found me. Till we meet again...take care, fellow IRCers!

APPENDIX A
DIRECTORY OF IRC CHANNELS

In this appendix you'll find an alphabetical list of brief, one-line channel descriptions—the basic information. The names of those channels discussed in greater detail in Chapter 6 are shown in bold below, and many additional channels are listed as well. Use this directory if you want a quick at-a-glance survey of what's on; for the *TV Guide* lover in you! (If only there were a remote control...)

Note: Due to the nature of IRC, some channels might be unavailable at the time you attempt to join them. However, others that have similar names or themes (or sometimes just different spellings) should work for you. Also note that the following list is not exhaustive, but it is a representative sampling that should keep most IRCers busy for a while!

Also keep in mind that any channel, listed in this book or elsewhere, can always be tried on either "regular" IRC servers or their Undernet counterparts. In other words, just because you see a channel name under the Undernet heading below doesn't mean you'll never find that channel on a non-Undernet server; it just means I first spotted it populated with people while I was on the Undernet. The same logic applies to channels listed under the "regular" IRC heading but not under the Undernet heading. Of course, some channels are present on both networks.

Regular IRC Channels

#abortion	Heated debates; can you think of a new argument?
#ad&d	The Dungeons and Dragons game.
#altmusic	About alternative music.
#Amiga	Commodore didn't survive but the Amiga thrives.
#AmigaGer	Like a German version of #Amiga.
#anarchism	
#appleIIgs	Yes, people still use the Apple IIgs computer.
#asian	
#astronomy	
#aussies	For lovers of Australia.
#australia	Also for lovers of Australia.
#bawel	For Indonesians.
#bdsm	Bondage talk and play.
#beijing	About the Chinese city, or Chinese culture.
#biblestud	Discussions about Bible study and Christianity.
#bisex	Bisexuals and friends.
#boggle	The popular word game.
#bolo	Discussion of this game.
#bondage	Same basic topic as #bdsm
#bored	General chat.
#Bosnia	
#boston	

#brasil	
#buddhist	About the worldwide religion/philosophy.
#c-64	About the Commodore 64 computer (old news to many).
#canada	
#chat	General chat.
#cheers	Not unlike the fictitious bar of NBC fame.
#china	
#chinese	
#Chomsky	About Noam Chomsky and his ideas/politics.
#christ	About Jesus and the religion formed in his wake.
#christian	About the global religion of Christianity.
#colombia	
#conquest	The fantasy game.
#cricket	For fans of the sport cricket.
#crossdres	Dedicated to transvestites.
#CS	Short for Czech/Slovak.
#Danmark/ #danmark	The Danish channel.
#darkrealm	On things gothic; sometimes vampires.
#dead	Has been a help channel in the past, but why the spooky name?
#depeche	About the band Depeche Mode.
#discuss	If it exists there must be some late-breaking news.
#disney	The empire known for Mickey, Goofy and long lines.

#doom	The video game; darn popular with these kids today.
#drugs	
#dutch	Intended for Dutch speakers.
#egypt	Intended for Egyptians or Egyptphiles.
#england/	
England	Devoted to Brits and Brits-in-spirit.
#erotica	General sex chat and activity.
#espanol	Related to the Spanish culture/language.
#Esperanto	Dedicated to the Esperanto language.
#EU-Opers	For European IRC operators.
#europe	
#falcon3.0	Discussion of this game.
#filipino	Related to the Philipines.
#florida	
#40plus	For those older than Jack Benny (i.e., over 39).
#42	A private channel version of #freenet.
#francais	French topics.
#francaise	French topics.
#france	French topics.
#freenet	Finnish speakers' hangout.
#gam	Geared toward gay Asian males and their friends.
#gaysex	Gay S&M chat and activity.
#GB/#gb	The Great Britain channel.
#Germany/	
#germany	For those into Deutsch culture, etc.

#gospel	General chat.
#gothic	On things gothic.
#guitar	About the instrument; English is not the default.
#hack	Geared mainly for hackers or those who feel they are.
#happy	General chat.
#heart	General chat.
#heathers	General chat.
#help	Ask IRC queries here; avoid asking on #Twilight_Zone.
#hk	On Hong Kong.
#hkfans	Usually Hong Kong students.
#hmong	
#hotsex	
#hottub	Popular friendly meeting space; flirting galore.
#hottub2	#hottub was so popular it spawned this spinoff.
#iceland	
#India/#india	
#Initgame	A virtual version of the Initials game.
#iran	
#IRCBar	Like a virtual Cheers. (Also try #ircbar spelling.)
#irchelp	A help channel for IRC users.
#IRC_Prefect	Another help channel available on occasion.
#ireland	
#islam	About the global religion.

#israel	
#italia	
#japan	
#jesus	About the famed religious leader, and Christianity.
#kampung	On Malaysia.
#kana	Finnish speakers' hangout.
#karate	For fans of the sport and philosophy of karate.
#kinky	General sex chat and activity.
#Klingon	Discussion related to these beings from *Star Trek*.
#kobe	Formed after the earthquake that devasted that city.
#korea	
#kuwait	
#laos	
#latvia	
#lesbos	For lesbians.
#limbaugh	About talk show host Rush.
#linpeople	Friendly help for Linux users.
#Linux	About the POSIX-compliant PC operating system.
#london	About the city in England.
#love	
#macintosh	About the computer born during that Orwell year.
#malaysia	On Malaysia.
#martial-a	For fans of the martial arts.
#melbourne	About the Australian city.

#moscow	
#movies	Discussion of moving pictures—you know, film.
#mtg	Chatting about the game called "Magic: The Gathering."
#muenster	About the friendly German town, not the cheese.
#nba	Basketball subjects.
#netsex	
#newcastle	About the city in England.
#nicecafe	General chat.
#nin	About the music group Nine Inch Nails.
#nippon	Another Japan channel.
#norway	
#os/2	About IBM's OS/2 operating system.
#p/g!	As in Grace Under Pressure; for fans of the band Rush.
#pakistan	
#palestine	
#penang	On Malaysia.
#penpal/ #penpals	
#perl	For computer mavens into this programming language.
#phonesex	
#phreak	There is a phenomenon known as phone phreaking.
#pinkfloyd	About the rock band Pink Floyd.
#poems	Where poets meet and sometimes read/critique poetry.
#poker	Continuous games are played.

#polska	For Polish persons or lovers of Poland's culture.
#prince	That is, the purple music man formerly known as.
#punk	The rock music form that won't die. Ask Green Day.
#rave	About rave music and culture.
#report	If it exists there must be some late-breaking news.
#RiskyBus	A virtual version of TV's *Jeopardy!* Q&A game.
#romance	For all you hopeless romantics.
#root	Mainly for those into the UNIX operating system.
#russian	
#seattle	
#seoul	
#sex	If you just answered M or F, you're on the wrong track.
#siam	For those from Thailand, or into Thai culture.
#silly	General chat.
#singapore	
#singles	
#Slovenia	
#soccer	For fans of the globally popular sport.
#socialism	
#spanking	
#startrek	
#starwars	
#studpoker	Continuous games of this variation on poker.
#Sweden/ #sweden	

#TahitiBar	Fun Finnish hangout; has some English WWW pages.
#taipei	Pertaining to the Taiwanese city.
#taiwan	
#talk2me	General chat.
#talk	General chat.
#teenlove	
#teens	
#texas	
#30plus	The channel for people over 30.
#35plus	For those 35 (like me, as I write this) and over.
#tibet	
#truthdare	A virtual version of the Truth or Dare game.
#turks	
#tw	Another Taiwanese-themed channel (try #taiwan too).
#12step	Recovery meetings.
#twilight	Discussion of the *Twilight Zone* TV show.
#Twilight_Zone	Mostly ops and server admins; not for help.
#unix	Dedicated to the UNIX operating system.
#usa	General chat.
#vampire	Go here when the urge bites you (or bytes you).
#veggies	For vegetarians.
#vidgames	Discussion of topics related to videogames.
#viet	Vietnamese themes.
#vietnight	Vietnamese themes.

#Wales	About this land, the western area of the U.K. island.
#warung	On Malaysia.
#wetsex	General sex chat and activity.
#wicca	Maybe you'll meet a witch here.
#www	World Wide Web is the subject of discussion.
#Zircon	About what many call the best X11 IRC client.

Undernet Channels

#30plus	
#acro	Rated R; "no under-17s unless accompanied by pervert!"
#asian	
#AynRand-Chat	The Objectivist Socializing Channel.
#AynRand/ #aynrand	The Objectivism Channel.
#bdsm	Self-described as "Bondage n stuff..."
#BRAZIL	
#callahans	A Callahans Bar, "for Puns & Floofenship."
#chaos	
#chat	They warn lamers, "Might as well kick yourself now."
#chatter	
#chatzone	
#ChitChat	
#conquest	"Ein Channel Internacional!" was their topic.
#CYBERSEX	

#DFW	
#Doom	About the Doom game (problems/hints/cheats/IHHD).
#Doomsday	To join this game, type **/msg DD Newplayer**
#doom][	About Doom's successor (problems/hints/cheats/IHHD).
#espanol	Viva Espana.
#Francais	They say "hobes le cidre breton est degueulasse:)"
#francaise	French-oriented subject matter, like the above.
#friends	
#Gamer	Latest in games (under construction; coming soon).
#gay	
#Hack	
#hamradio	Talk about ham radio, the Amateur Radio BBS, etc.
#help	For getting help about IRC.
#hotsex	
#Hottub	
#IRCBar	
#ireland	
#islam	The religion/philosophy. "Assalamualaikum!"
#linpeople	Friendly help for Linux.
#Linux	About the POSIX-compliant PC operating system.
#mormon	The Church of Jesus Christ of Latter-day Saints.
#Net.Info	
#netsex	
#Podium	Home of the Internet Roundtable speaker series/show.

#poker	Welcome to the Undernet Poker Channel!
#popcorn	
#RiskyBus	
#romance	
#root	
#secrets	"The strongest friendship is built with secrets."
#spanking	Adult Spanking Forum. "C'mon in!," they exclaim.
#talk2me	Channel designed "for [the] socially challenged."
#telerama	Their topic: "A friendly suburb of Pittsburgh."
#viet	
#wasteland	For Undernet help; Undernet operators' hangout.

APPENDIX B
IRC SERVERS

In this appendix you'll find addresses of both "regular" IRC servers and Undernet servers, broken down by geographic region.

Regular IRC Servers

The "regular" IRC server entries include the domain name of the server followed by a more specific geographic location, when available. Note that IRC server ports are assumed to be 6667 unless otherwise noted below. Most IRC clients will assume 6667 as a default if you do not indicate a port number.

United States

merlin.acf-lab.alaska.edu	Alaska
cs-pub.bu.edu	Boston, MA
csa.bu.edu	Boston, MA
irc.bu.edu	Boston, MA
nova.unix.portal.com	California
irc.colorado.edu*	Colorado

*Try port 6665 or 6666 if you can't connect

irc.math.ufl.edu	Florida
irc.uiuc.edu	Illinois
copper.ucs.indiana.edu	Indiana
sluaxa.slu.edu	Louisiana
irc-2.mit.edu	Massachusetts
organ.ctr.columbia.edu	New York
hobbes.catt.ncsu.edu	North Carolina
irc.csos.orst.edu	Oregon
irc.duq.edu	Pennsylvania
irc.bga.com	Texas
irc.math.byu.edu	Utah
poe.acc.virginia.edu	Virginia

Canada

sol.csd.unb.ca

Europe

bim.itc.univie.ac.at	Austria
olymp.wu-wien.ac.at 6666	Austria
sokrates.informatik.uni-kl.de	Denmark
irc.funet.fi	Finland
cismhp.univ-lyon1.fr	France
disuns2.epfl.ch	
irc.nada.kth.se	

Australia

ircserver.cltr.uq.oz.au

jello.qabc.uq.oz.au

Undernet Servers

The entries for Undernet servers are organized a little differently than the entries for regular IRC servers above. The first line of each entry is the server's domain name (which is often all you need to know), but for some entries, an alternative numeric form (to try if the name in the first line does not work) is provided on the next line. The last line of each entry gives the physical location of the server.

United States

Some of these servers may also run on ports 7000/7777.

Pasadena.CA.US.undernet.org 6667
(or 131.215.48.152 6667)
California Institute of Technology, Pasadena, CA

Norman.OK.US.undernet.org 6667
(or 129.15.22.33 6667)
University of Oklahoma, Norman, OK

Boston.MA.US.undernet.org 6667
(or 129.10.22.11 6667)
Northeastern University, Boston, MA

Albany.NY.US.undernet.org 6667
(or 128.213.5.17 6667)
Rensselaer Polytechnic Institute, Troy, NY

Manhattan.KS.US.undernet.org 6667
(or 129.130.8.12 6667)
Kansas State University, Manhattan, KS

Milwaukee.WI.US.undernet.org 6667
(or 140.104.4.169 6667)
Carroll College, Waukesha, WI

Ames.IA.US.undernet.org 6667
(or 129.186.22.72 6667)
Iowa State University, Ames, IA

StGeorge.UT.US.undernet.org 6667
(or 144.38.16.2 6667)
Dixie College, St. George, UT

Tampa.FL.US.undernet.org 6667
(or 131.247.31.19 6667)
University of South Florida, Tampa, FL

Davis.CA.US.undernet.org 6667
(or 128.120.2.8 6667)
Davis, CA

Austin.TX.US.undernet.org 6667
(or 128.83.162.106 6667)
Austin, TX

Canada

This server may also run on ports 7000/7777.

Montreal.QU.CA.undernet.org 6667
(or 132.207.12.13 6667)
Montreal, Quebec, Canada

Mexico

This server may also run on ports 7000/7777.

Puebla.MX.undernet.org 6666
(or 140.148.4.100 6666)
Universidad de las Americas, Puebla, Mexico

Chile

This server may also run on ports 7000/7777.

Santiago.CL.undernet.org 6667
(or 146.83.1.1 6667)
Reuna, Red Universitaria Nacional

Europe

Most of these servers also run on port 7000.

Lausanne.CH.EU.undernet.org 6667
(or 130.223.201.6 6667)
University of Lausanne, Institute of Anatomy, Lausanne, Switzerland

Crete.GR.EU.undernet.org 6666
(or 147.52.16.1 6666)
University of Crete, Computer Science Department, Greece

Caen.FR.EU.undernet.org 7000
(or 192.93.101.16 7000)
Ecole Nationale Superieure d'Ingenieurs de Caen, France

Paderborn.DE.EU.undernet.org 6667
(or 131.234.128.204 6667)
University of Paderborn, Pderborn, Germany

Delft.NL.EU.undernet.org 6667
(or 130.161.188.188 6667)
Netherlands

Vienna.AT.EU.undernet.org 6667
(or 127.208.3.30 6667)
Vienna, Austria

Ljubljana.Si.Eu.undernet.org 6668
(or 193.2.1.67 6668)
Ljubljana, Slovenia

Oslo.No.EU.undernet.org 6667
(or 128.39.107.112 6667)
NKI Ingenioerhoegskolen, Oslo, Norway

Gothenburg.Se.EU.undernet.org 6667
(or 129.16.79.30 6667)
Chalmers Tekniska Lekskola, Gothenburg, Sweden

Krakow.PL.EU.undernet.org 7000
(or 149.156.96.9 7000)
Krakow, Poland

Uxbridge.UK.EU.undernet.org 6667
(or 134.83.32.97 6667)
Brunel University, Uxbridge, London, UK

Asia

Taipei.tw.undernet.org 6667
(or 140.109.103.204 6667)
Taipei, Taiwan

Australia

Wollongong.NSW.AU.undernet.org 6667
(or 130.130.64.75 6667)
U of Wollongong, Dept. of Computer Science, Wollongong, Australia

APPENDIX C
ABOUT THE ONLINE COMPANION

Ready to chat it up? the *Internet Chat Online Companion* plumbs the depths of IRC and IRC-related resources on the Internet, serving as an informative tool as well as an annotated software library. It aids in your exploration of chat servers and channels by providing you with links to useful IRC (both EFnet—"regular" IRC—and Undernet) FAQs, guides and tutorials. Check out the links to various chat-related WWW pages, or take a look at Internet Theatre, where Net denizens perform such cyberchat productions as *An IRC Channel Named Desire* or *PCbeth—an IBM clone of Macbeth*. You're never out of the loop with this online companion.

Also, the *Internet Chat Online Companion* hyperlinks to the channels, chat-related newsgroups and other resources referenced in Chapter 6 of the *Internet Chat Quick Tour* book. Just click on the reference name and jump directly to the server or resource you're interested in.

Perhaps one of the most valuable features of the *Internet Chat Online Companion* is its Software Archive. Here, you'll be able to download the latest versions of software mentioned in the *Internet Chat Quick Tour* that is freely available on the Internet. This software includes Macintosh and Windows chat clients such as Ircle, Homer, Winirc and Wsirc, which allow your computer to communicate with IRC servers;

plus Internet essentials such as Fetch and WS_FTP, which make it easy to transfer files to and from your computer. With Ventana Online's helpful descriptions of the software, you'll know exactly what you're getting and why—so you won't download software just to find you have no use for it.

The *Internet Chat Online Companion* also links you to the Ventana Library, where you'll find useful press and jacket information on a variety of Ventana Press offerings. Plus, you have access to a wide selection of exciting new releases and coming attractions. In addition, Ventana's Online Library allows you to order the books you want.

The *Internet Chat Online Companion* represents Ventana Online's ongoing commitment to offering the most dynamic and exciting products possible. And soon Ventana Online will be adding more services, including an IRC server, more multimedia supplements, searchable indexes and sections of the *Internet Chat Quick Tour* reproduced and hyperlinked to the Internet resources they reference.

To access the online companion, connect via the World Wide Web to **http://www.vmedia.com/icqt.html**

GLOSSARY

Bot An online software "robot." Bots typically operate from a program or script that is designed to either generate dialogue, or recognize it, or both. When they are not blindly banned by a server, bots often serve as automated knowledge dispensers, responding to user requests by providing information or files. They can also be used to keep a channel active automatically. Avoid the flooding bot variety.

BTW Abbreviation for *By The Way;* common on the Net.

C U l8r Typical IRCspeak, in place of *see you later;* may be used before leaving a channel.

Channel The virtual space where IRC users converse. There are typically thousands on IRC at any time.

Client The program you run in order to connect to an IRC server. Provides the interface you use to talk on channels, send commands, save logs of your sessions, etc.

Direct connection A connection where your personal computer is directly hooked to the Internet. (As opposed to a shell account, which see.) Both types of connections can be used to gain access to IRC, but the direct kind may mean a bit more work for the user (in return for more flexibility, in most cases).

d00d   Typical IRCspeak, in place of *dude.*

Flooding   Spewing out unwanted character strings (e.g., garbage, or canned sentences) on a channel. Disrupts channel activity, hence abhorred by most IRCers. Often carried out via flooding bots.

FTF   Widely used Net abbreviation for *Face To Face,* usually referring to a live meeting as opposed to one on IRC. Also F2F.

Hir   A gender-free compression of *his or her.* Sometimes used in conversation, more often in written documents posted on various areas of the Net.

Homer   A Mac-based graphical interface to IRC. Could be the wave of the future for IRC interactions. Program is available on the Net (e.g., from sumex-aim.stanford.edu in the Macintosh directory, under Communications).

IMHO   Widely used Net abbreviation for *In My Humble Opinion.*

IRC   You mean you've read this entire book and still don't know what this means?:-) Internet Relay Chat. Like CB radio for cyberspace, it is the system by which Net users around the world can talk in real time with each other.

IRCers   My own slang for the people who use IRC.

IRL   A Net abbreviation for *In Real Life,* as in an honest-to-God real-life rendezvous with someone (perhaps someone you met on IRC). *See also* FTF.

Kewl   Typical IRCspeak, in place of *cool.*

Kicked   Kicked off an IRC channel. Ops can do this.

Lagged   If someone on a channel tells you you're lagged, your text input is taking a long time to be output on others' screens. Can be due to network-caused delays; sometimes switching to another IRC server can alleviate or lessen your "lag time."

Lamer   IRCspeak meaning someone who is, or acts, uncool. As in, "That guy is such a *lamer*!!"

Newsgroup   One of the bulletin boards on USENET.

Nickname   Also known as a *nick*. The name by which you will be known to other people on IRC; almost always different than any part of your e-mail address. Each line of text you send to a channel will be prefixed by your nick on other users' screens. It's considered taboo to duplicate another user's nick.

Op   Short for operator.

Oper   Short for operator.

Operator   A *channel operator* (also known as a *chanop* or just *op*) is the IRC user "in charge" of a channel. The first person to join a channel (i.e., its creator) automatically gets channel operator status, and can either "rule" alone or share ruling status with anyone he or she wants. A chanop usually can kick people off the channel. An operator can be spotted online by the @ next to his/her nickname in the list generated by a /names command, or an @ by the channel name in the output of a /whois command.

An *IRC operator* maintains the IRC network as a whole, and does not deal with specific channel issues.

Page   A node in the World Wide Web (which see). A collection of information that includes text, plus links to other pages (in most cases), and sometimes even graphics, audio or video elements. One clicks on a page's links to jump to other pages; a series of leaps from page to page is commonly known as *surfing, Net surfing* or *Web surfing.*

"Regular" IRC   I sometimes use this term (also "standard" IRC) to distinguish the non-Undernet world of IRC from that of the Undernet.

Server   A computer site that actually runs IRC; you connect to it (via your client) so that you can participate. You could think of a server as the conduit between you and the other IRC users around the world, each of whom is also using a server (there are many) to connect to IRC.

s/he   Compressed version of *she or he.*

Shell account   An indirect Internet connection, where you must dial in to institution-X's computer, which has the direct connection for you to use. Shell accounts tend to cost a certain amount per month to use—usually a flat fee plus a possible hourly charge. However, some institutions (e.g., colleges and some commercial enterprises) let their students/employees have free shell accounts.

SLIP   Short for *Serial Line Internet Protocol.* A protocol used to make a temporary direct connection to the Internet over a phone line.

str8   Typical IRCspeak, in place of *straight* (as in sexual orientation).

System message   Text that appears on a channel that is not generated by one of the users on that channel; for example, an announcement of someone entering or leaving that channel. Also may refer to information generated by an IRC server, such as the server's welcome message (which see).

Undernet   Basically an "alternate universe" to "regular" IRC. Uses a different set of servers than standard IRC, but the basic operation is the same. Some Undernet channels might not be present on regular IRC, and vice versa. Also thought by some users to be a more friendly universe than regular IRC.

USENET   Basically a collection of electronic bulletin boards (each of which is called a newsgroup). There are about a dozen groups that deal with IRC issues.

Welcome message   Information generated by a server when you first connect to that server. Typically includes the rules and regulations, if any, for that server; for instance, whether bots are banned.

World Wide Web   Also known as WWW or simply the Web. A hypertext system that consists of many pages, stored on various computers all over the world. This book lists some of the many Web pages dedicated to IRC-related subjects.

BIBLIOGRAPHY

There are other publications—books, magazines, papers, etc.—that discuss IRC either directly or indirectly. Here's a list to get you going. (By some strange coincidence, all of the authors' last names below begin with R; it's not on purpose, I swear.)

Reed, Darren. *A Discussion on Computer Network Conferencing.* 1992. Provides a theoretical background on why conferencing systems such as IRC are a good thing. Available via FTP at nic.ddn.mil in the rfc directory, as rfc1324.txt.

Reid, Elisabeth. *Electropolis: Communications and Community on Internet Relay Chat.* Honors thesis, Dept. of History, University of Melbourne, Australia, 1991. A thesis focusing on IRC, particularly its social and psychological implications. Widely available (distributed and referenced) on the Net.

Rheingold, Howard. *The Virtual Community.* Reading, MA: Addison-Wesley Publishing Company, 1993. Discussion of IRC centers on its social implications. Also includes some keen perceptions about IRC as well as humorous anecdotes and folklore.

Robinson, M. Virtual Cafe. *Axcess*, Vol. 2, No. 4, 1994. PO Box 9309, San Diego, CA 92169. Bimonthly. Profiles some of the people who meet on IRC; mainly geared towards GenXers (or anyone who identifies with a lost generation—take your pick). Focus is on the cafe-like channels, and how they enable cafe society to live on in the virtual world of the Net.

Rose, Donald. *Minding Your Cybermanners on the Internet*. Indianapolis: Alpha Books, 1994. Covers all areas of online etiquette, including chat; also sheds light on some areas of cybermanners folklore.

INDEX

COLOPHON

This book was developed on a Macintosh Quadra 650. All pages were produced in Aldus PageMaker 5.0. Some graphics were produced or edited using Adobe Illustrator 5.0. Chapter titles are set in Anna. The body text is Palatino with Futura subheads, sidebars and tables. The title of the book (on the cover and title pages) is set in Michelangelo. Page proofs were output to a Hewlett-Packard LaserJet 4M Plus and final film output was produced using a Linotronic 330.

Internet Resources

The Windows Internet Tour Guide, Second Edition
$29.95, 424 pages, illustrated

This runaway bestseller has been updated to include Enhanced Mosaic, the hot new Web reader, along with graphical software for e-mail, file downloading, newsreading and more. Noted for its down-to-earth documentation, the new edition features expanded listings and a look at new Net developments.
BONUS: Includes three companion disks.

Internet E-Mail Quick Tour
$14.00, 152 pages, illustrated

Whether it's the Internet or an online service, most people use their connections primarily for electronic messaging. This all-in-one guide to getting it right includes tips on software, security, style and Netiquette. Also included: how to obtain an e-mail account, useful addresses, interesting mailing lists and more!

Publishing on the Internet, Windows Edition
$34.95, 400 pages, illustrated

Successful publishing for the Internet requires an understanding of "nonlinear" presentation as well as specialized software. Both are here. Learn how HTML builds the hot links that let readers choose their own paths—and how to use effective design to drive a message or theme. The companion CD-ROM contains Ventana Mosaic™, an HTML editor, a graphics viewer, templates, conversion software and more. Available in April.

Internet Virtual Worlds Quick Tour

$14.00, 150 pages, illustrated

Learn to locate and master real-time interactive communication forums and games by participating in the virtual worlds of MUD (Multi-User Dimension) and MOO (MUD Object-Oriented). *Internet Virtual Worlds Quick Tour* introduces users to the basic functions by defining different categories (individual, interactive and both) and detailing standard protocols. Also revealed is the insider's lexicon of these mysterious cyberworlds. Available in March.

Internet Roadside Attractions

$29.95, 384 pages, illustrated

Why take the word of one when you can get a quorum? Seven experienced Internauts—teachers and bestselling authors—share their favorite Web sites, Gophers, FTP sites, chats, games, newsgroups and mailing lists. Organized alphabetically by category for easy browsing with in-depth descriptions. The companion CD-ROM contains the entire text of the book, hyperlinked for off-line browsing and online Web-hopping.

Walking the World Wide Web

$29.95, 360 pages, illustrated

Enough of lengthy listings! This tour features more than 300 memorable Web sites, with in-depth descriptions of what's special about each. Includes international sites, exotic exhibits, entertainment, business and more. The companion CD-ROM contains Ventana Mosaic™ and a hyperlinked version of the book, providing live links when you log on to the Internet.

Books marked with this logo include a free Internet *Online Companion*™, featuring archives of free utilities plus a software archive and links to other Internet resources.

Insightful Guides

The Official America Online for Windows Membership Kit & Tour Guide, Second Edition

$27.95, 568 pages, illustrated

Experience the delights of online communications and AOL's easy graphical interface. The second edition of this bestseller offers a glimpse of AOL's fresh new interface, reorganized services and Internet access. Tips on saving time and money online are liberally spiced with behind-the-scenes stories and online experiences. The companion disk includes the latest version of AOL's starter software, one month free membership and 20 hours of free online time (new members only).

America Online's Internet, Windows Edition

$24.95, 328 pages, illustrated

AOL members can now slide onto the Infobahn with a mere mouse click. This quick-start for AOL Internet newcomers explains e-mail, downloading files, reading newsgroups and joining mailing lists. The companion disk includes AOL software and ten hours of free online time (for new members only).

Voodoo Windows

$19.95, 312 pages, illustrated

Work Windows wizardry with productivity-enhancing tips. Organized by subject, this book offers a wealth of Windows techniques, shortcuts and never-before-published tricks that will streamline your daily tasks and save time. A great reference for beginners and experienced users alike.

Windows, Word & Excel Office Companion, Second Edition
$21.95, 694 pages, illustrated

With more than 100,000 copies sold, this groundbreaking title eliminates the need for newcomers to purchase three separate books. Three sections offer easy introductions to Microsoft's industry-leading software: Windows™ through Version 3.1, Word through Version 6 and Excel through Version 5. An extensive index makes this down-to-earth guide to basic commands and features an easy reference that saves time, money and valuable desktop acreage.

The Windows Shareware 500
$39.95, 456 pages, illustrated

The best Windows shareware available, from thousands of contenders. Includes utilities, sounds, fonts, icons, games, clip art, multimedia and more. **BONUS:** Four companion disks: three that feature top-rated programs and an America Online membership disk. Includes 10 hours free online time (for new members only).

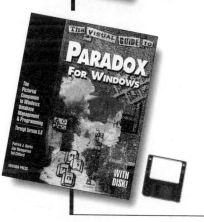

The Visual Guide to Paradox for Windows
$29.95, 692 pages, illustrated

A uniquely pictorial approach to Paradox! Hundreds of examples and illustrations show how to achieve complex database development with simple drag-and-drop techniques. Users learn how to access and modify database files, use Form and Report Designers and Experts, program with ObjectPal and more—all with icons, buttons, graphics and OLE. The companion disk contains sample macros, forms, reports, tables, queries and a ready-to-use database.

Welcome to Ventana Online.

Do you have an Internet connection? If so, Ventana Online is your electronic Internet companion, offering a wealth of opportunities to enhance your Internet travels.

Download the latest free version of Mosaic. Sample its "helper" applications and other excellent freeware programs.

Browse Ventana's *Online Companions*™ featuring hyperlinked sample chapters from our books, plus updated software and links to valuable Internet resources. And we'll tell you about lots of great sites on the Net, including our "Nifty Site of the Week."

So many things to do and places to go! And with Ventana Online, you're never "lost in cyberspace." So visit Ventana Online. We're just a URL away!

Ventana Online
http://www.vmedia.com/

VENTANA
ONLINE

TITLE	ISBN	Quantity	Price	Total
America Online's Internet, Windows Version	1-56604-176-7	_____ x	$24.95 =	$ _____
Internet Chat Quick Tour	1-56604-223-2	_____ x	$14.00 =	$ _____
Internet E-Mail Quick Tour	1-56604-220-8	_____ x	$14.00 =	$ _____
Internet Roadside Attractions	1-56604-193-7	_____ x	$29.95 =	$ _____
Internet Virtual Worlds Quick Tour	1-56604-222-4	_____ x	$14.00 =	$ _____
The Official America Online For Windows Membership Kit & Tour Guide, 2nd Edition	1-56604-128-7	_____ x	$27.95 =	$ _____
Publishing on the Internet, Windows Edition	1-56604-229-1	_____ x	$34.95 =	$ _____
The Visual Guide to Paradox for Windows	1-56604-150-3	_____ x	$29.95 =	$ _____
Voodoo Windows	1-56604-005-1	_____ x	$19.95 =	$ _____
Walking the World Wide Web	1-56604-208-9	_____ x	$29.95 =	$ _____
The Windows Internet Tour Guide, 2nd Edition	1-56604-174-0	_____ x	$29.95 =	$ _____
The Windows Shareware 500	1-56604-045-0	_____ x	$39.95 =	$ _____
Windows, Word & Excel Office Companion, 2nd Edition	1-56604-083-3	_____ x	$21.95 =	$ _____

To order any Ventana Press title, complete this order form and mail or fax it to us, with payment, for quick shipment.

Subtotal = $ _____
Shipping = $ _____
TOTAL = $ _____

SHIPPING:

For all standard orders, please ADD $4.50/first book, $1.35/each additional.
For "two-day air," ADD $8.25/first book, $2.25/each additional.
For orders to Canada, ADD $6.50/book.
For orders sent C.O.D., ADD $4.50 to your shipping rate.
North Carolina residents must ADD 6% sales tax.
International orders require additional shipping charges.

Name _____ Daytime telephone _____

Company _____

Address (No PO Box) _____

City _____ State _____ Zip _____

____ Payment enclosed ____VISA ____MC Acc't # _____ Exp. date _____

Exact name on card _____ Signature _____

Check your local bookstore or software retailer for these and other bestselling titles, or call toll free 800/7 43-5369

Mail to: Ventana Press, PO Box 2468, Chapel Hill, NC 27515 ☎ 800/743-5369 Fax 919/942-1140